The 20-Month

Legend

MY BABY BOY'S FIGHT WITH CANCER

STEVE TATE

SAVIO
REPVBLIC

A SAVIO REPUBLIC BOOK
An Imprint of Post Hill Press

ISBN: 978-1-68261-512-6
ISBN (eBook): 978-1-68261-513-3

The 20-Month Legend
My Baby Boy's Fight with Cancer
© 2018 by Steve Tate

Cover Design by Tricia Principe, principedesign.com

posthillpress.com
New York • Nashville
Published in the United States of America

CONTENTS

PREFACE

*B*efore you dive into reading this book, I want to give you a snapshot of twenty months in my life so that I don't bore you to tears. If, by the end of this preface, you still have no interest in me or my story then it's okay to part ways and move on. There's no commitment or obligation—a clean break is still manageable. We don't have any kids together, so it's not going to get ugly.

In March of 2015, I found myself in an operating room with my wife as she was giving birth. Don't worry, this is not another book reflecting on life lessons while becoming a parent for the first time. You can stop pressing the panic button. I had already been a parent three times over. I was a pro at this parenting thing. This time, my wife was giving birth to three human beings. Yep, that's right: our family was going from three crazy children to six.

We managed to juggle all of these kids. No, we didn't literally juggle them, although that would definitely catch your attention and probably get some publicity. I managed to keep my sanity through the first nine months of their lives. Although I envisioned my life would be over, I actually felt an insane amount of joy from parenting these babies and watching them grow. Until life threw us another curve ball.

You'll see that I use an unhealthy amount of sports analogies and references. But that's because I'm a washed-up, has-been collegiate football player. At one point in my life, I was an extremely successful football player from Utah: a three-year, all-conference starter and captain at the University of Utah where I played safety. Actually, I was an overachieving football player who probably defied the odds, but that first line sounds way better. That was all before this whole

Dad bod took over. I blame gravity. I moved on from my football playing days and found incredible happiness raising children with the girl of my dreams, who happens to be my high-school sweetheart. I thought I had life all figured out, until...

At nine months old, one of our triplets was diagnosed with a brain tumor that consumed a third of his brain. He was later diagnosed with a type of brain cancer that affects one in every three-million children with tumors.

In the midst of this incredibly hard time, somehow my wife and I were able to find hope. We found joy in moments that weren't supposed to be joyful. If you are facing a challenging time in your life and need help finding hope, keep reading and follow our twenty-month journey. We have found, through a social media audience that is approaching 80,000 followers, that people from all demographics, religions, and cultures are drawn to this story of hope and love.

I feel like our story needs to be told. Our entire journey was guided by impressions, or instincts, if you will. We relied on many of those instincts at the initial diagnosis and up until the very last day of this journey. They seemed to have done me well to this point, so I followed the instinct to write this book. My honest wish is to provide perspective to anyone who reads it. Unfortunately, perspective is usually gained during moments of tragedy or crisis, so my hope is that people read this book and change their perspective—free from tragedy or crisis. Let our journey be the turning point for your desire to live life with more purpose, or to parent your children with more patience and love.

I have never written a book before. However, I do get extreme pleasure from making people laugh, cry, smile, or even cringe. In Jimmy Valvano's famous speech during his final days of fighting cancer, he said, "If you laugh, you think, and you cry, that's a full day. That's a heck of a day. You do that seven days a week, you're going to have something special." You may find my style of writing quirky, but I can guarantee you that it will make you laugh, think and cry. What else do you need in a book?

Savanna, baby Bo, and me during my football days at the University of Utah.

FOREWORD

"Wait, I know that voice. I think I went to high school with this guy," I remember saying to my brother as we drove back to our family's house on the icy Salt Lake City roads after some Christmas shopping. The University of Utah football game had just ended. We were listening to the postgame show on the car radio.

My brother and I were both back visiting for Christmas. I was living in Los Angeles pursuing a career in screenwriting and my brother was living in Austin, Texas. We were taking a little break from home, from all that delightful bickering and sibling infighting that happens around Christmas. I always figured we'd outgrow such hostilities, but I guess certain things are just forever a part of the holiday season—as much a tradition as presents under the tree, Santa Claus, and caroling. My family had recently lost our father to Lou Gehrig's disease, and we were still in the process of learning how to navigate events like Christmas without spiraling into sadness comas. So things were additionally tense back at the house. We were self-medicating with lots of screaming, followed by lots of crying, followed by lots of eating of Frosty-the-Snowman-shaped sugar cookies, then more screaming.

"Yeah, that's Steve Tate. I went to high school with him," I said with pride in my voice. It's nice when one of your friends becomes famous and you can say, *"Hey, I know that guy,"* hoping that simply by knowing someone cooler than you are, you will suddenly, somehow be a little cooler yourself. At the very least, I was hoping my brother would be impressed that I knew someone on the radio.

"I don't care. Drive faster. I've got to pee," my brother said, unimpressed.

But *I* was impressed. It's hard to get on the radio.

Aside from being on the radio, I had no idea what Steve had been up to. We had grown apart since high school—fading away from each other as people do. I knew that he had gone on a Mormon mission and played college football for Utah State and then for the University of Utah. Meanwhile, I had done the exact opposite: heading to college at hippie Berkeley, then returning home to care for my sick dad, before heading back to California to pursue a risky writing career in Los Angeles. I remember thinking, *Man, Steve sounds like he's doing awesome. Good for him.*

After hearing him on the radio, I was curious what else Steve had been up to over the years. Instead of tracking down his phone number and calling him up for a hang and catch up, I turned to creepy, old Facebook and Google. After all, why reach out to people in person when you can quietly stalk them online?

My hypothesis that Steve was doing awesome proved to be accurate. It looked like he had built an absolutely idyllic life for himself, living an almost Norman Rockwell-type existence. He had married his high school sweetheart, Savanna, and had three beautiful children. Savanna and I were actually pals in high school. We had been Student Body Officers (SBOs) together at Skyline High. Neither of us were as athletic as Steve, who was the school's starting quarterback, so we were more into planning dances and cracking jokes at assemblies than throwing touchdowns.

It was good to see that they were both doing so well. I was incredibly happy for them.

After Christmas, I went back to Los Angeles to continue pursuing my writing career. At the time, I was living a fairly lonely existence, too focused on my writing to care about things like dating, or owning a dog, or personal hygiene. I'm a huge Utah Jazz fan. But only a handful of Jazz games are nationally televised out in Los Angeles. I thus decided to treat myself to the NBA League Pass. I'd watch most games alone on my couch while sending out angry Tweets about the team's performance.

As I tweeted my life away, I happened to notice that Steve was also an avid fan and would send out similarly angry tweets. So, we started conversing about the Jazz over Twitter. We were a couple of dudes who had reunited through our mutual dissatisfaction of our favorite sports team. It was nice. Social media mostly sucks, but occasionally you're fortunate enough to reconnect with an old pal and give your friendship a second chance, a sort of rebirth.

After more loneliness and lots of Jazz games, things finally started to go my way career-wise. I had written a book called *Home is Burning* about my family caring for my dad while he was fighting Lou Gehrig's disease. It was finally getting published and the movie rights had sold to New Line with Miles Teller attached to star. Steve and Savanna read the book when it came out and reached out to me over Facebook with some incredibly kind, heartfelt words.

Prompted by their kind words, I decided to treat myself to another light stalking of Steve and Savanna's social media accounts.

I assumed everything was still great in their lives. But then I noticed something massive had happened to them. Savanna had given birth to triplets. That's right, they doubled their kid-count from three to six just like that. I remember telling my kid-less friends out in Los Angeles about it. "I have a friend who just had triplets. And they already have three kids. Isn't that crazy?" I could barely keep myself fed and alive, and here Steve and Savanna were now taking care of six children? I was amazed.

But I knew if there was anyone who could handle such a life-altering challenge, it was Steve and Savanna. They were both so tough, so resilient. I remember in high school Savanna had quietly battled and beaten thyroid cancer. And Steve was known as being an absolute beast of a competitor on the football field. When Steve had transferred from Utah State to the University of Utah, he had changed positions from quarterback to safety, showing a certain adaptability and willingness to accept a new challenge. They were strong, hardworking, malleable people. Six kids would be hectic and intense, but I knew they could do it.

Then, as they appeared to be settling into their new lives, Steve shared some sad news over social media. One of the triplets, Hayes, had been diagnosed with an extremely rare form of brain cancer. The news was devastating. Anyone who has ever seen a loved one battle cancer—or any other ailment for that matter—knows what a terrible, uphill fight it is.

I was in shock once again. I couldn't believe that something so bad had happened to such good people. I couldn't believe the Rockwellian image of the Tates was now tarnished by the evils of cancer.

But again, I knew that Steve and Savanna would adapt to the new challenge and go through it with the poise and bravery that most of us don't possess. Some people cower under pressure, while others give a gladiator-esque scream and charge toward it. I knew Steve and Savanna would be gladiators. And because he was the son of such strong, spirited parents, I knew that Hayes would be too. I knew that he had inherited their toughness. I knew the whole family would power through this tragedy with an immense amount of courage and strength. I knew that they would fight with everything they had.

And they did.

Steve and Savanna fought with the strength and love than only a parent can summon up. And Hayes battled through hardships greater than anyone his age was built to endure. And while they fought, they showed the power of hope, the power of family, the power of love.

Everybody handles tragedy differently. Some people choose to go through it quietly, in an almost silent reserve, while others place a megaphone up to their mouth and shout every little detail to the world. When my dad was sick, I chose the latter. I revealed everything in my book. Looking back, I probably revealed too much, as was evident when my brother asked, "Did you really need to mention that I'm not circumcised?" But I figured that my story could be a snapshot that could help other people going through something similar.

Steve and Savanna have chosen a similar openness with Hayes's battle with childhood cancer. They have dedicated their Facebook and Instagram accounts to showing us all, firsthand, what it's like to go through such an intense and heartbreaking struggle. And now Steve has written this beautiful book—a book that has so much heart and love in it that it's practically bursting through its seams, a book that is an amazing tribute to an amazingly brave little boy, Hayes.

I'm personally glad Steve and Savanna were fearless enough to share their story. Such intense openness isn't easy. It's hard to let people in—to give an almost voyeuristic window into your life, your soul. But doing so will unquestionably provide readers with a look inside the battle with such a terrible disease. It will explore all the grieving, all the sadness, all the heartbreak, mixed with the occasional moments of levity, that a family goes through during a tragedy. We all learn through struggle, and I have no doubt in my mind that, by sharing his family's struggle, Steve will help others going through similar trials and tribulations to go through them with analogous bravery and strength.

So I thank Steve for writing this book. I thank him for his openness. I thank him for all the support and guidance that his book will undoubtedly provide for others. Thank you, Steve, and thank you, Savanna. Thanks for being such shining examples to us all. And most of all, thank you for being such great parents to Hayes and the rest of your children.

Dan Marshall
June 2017

1

ULTRASOUND

"Well, you guys sure know how to make babies." That's how she put it.

"Babies?" I asked the doctor. "You mean there's more than one?"

"There are three babies in here," she responded. I felt all the color in my face drain away, my hands began to tingle, and my head was about to hit the floor. I almost passed out. The nurse ran out the door to get me some water.

We sat in utter astonishment. The doctor asked whether we wanted to hear the heartbeats. I was hesitant. I wasn't sure, I wasn't even sure where I was at that moment. *How did this happen?* I thought. *There is no way we can be having triplets. That's only make believe, like unicorn-type material.* Triplets only existed on television. My mind wandered to that terrible reality show *Jon & Kate Plus 8*. I got hives watching that show. All those screaming babies running around the house gave me IBS symptoms. I am kind of a neat freak, so three babies and neatness don't typically go hand in hand. Plus, we have three older kids. Now you see why I almost passed out—six kids is no joke. That's freak show material.

It was the eight-week ultrasound, and my wife Savanna had been feeling really nauseous, much more nauseous than she had with the previous three pregnancies. I still sat in silence as Savanna agreed to hear the heartbeats. The physician moved the wand around to the first baby and we heard a beautiful, healthy heartbeat.

"That's Baby A," she said. It became real. It started to sink in. She moved the wand a little more until we heard the second heartbeat.

"Here is Baby B," she said pointing to the screen. We listened to the puttering. I felt connected. They were mine. She wiggled the wand around toward the third shadow on the screen. I could tell she was struggling to identify the exact location. She tried several times before letting us know that the third baby, Baby C, didn't have a heartbeat.

"It's pretty typical in pregnancies with multiples", she said. "I'd say it's a 50/50 chance that this baby develops enough to have a heartbeat."

The doctor cleaned up and left the room. I sat in shock. I didn't say a word to Savanna. I would've cried if I had the energy or a thought in my head. I was numb. We sat there a few minutes before leaving the room to set up our next appointment. The doctor wanted to see us again in two weeks to see whether the third baby had developed a heartbeat.

As we turned to leave the clinic, the nurses were all staring at us. They all knew—word had traveled fast. We walked down the hallway and many of them said congratulations. I tried to find words to respond, but there was nothing going on upstairs. We were walking in slow motion and everyone else was in normal mode. We were about to have six freaking kids.

Savanna and I had driven to the clinic in separate cars since I had come from an appointment. I'm a financial advisor, but I was about to become a professional dad. I had a fifteen-minute drive back to the office. I cried. I don't remember the last time I had cried, but I wept like a baby. Don't get me wrong, I love kids. But making the jump from three kids to six kids is like getting called up to the majors out of high school.

I wasn't ready to tell anybody quite yet. Do you blame me? People had always identified me as "Steve Tate, the former player at the University of Utah." Well, that was about to change. I was now going to be "Steve Tate, the man who went for baby number four and got triplets." I could barely think, let alone have an adult conversation that involved others realizing my life was about to change entirely. In fact, the term "changing" would require me to actually still be alive. For all I knew, my life was over. Needless to say, I didn't get much work done that afternoon. I couldn't even make eye contact with clients.

I finished up my meetings for the day and headed home. Savanna and I hadn't talked since the Doctor's visit, but we mustered up some type of conversation. It was enough of a discussion to agree that telling our kids was a necessary step. The kids knew we were pregnant. They were so excited to have a new baby brother or sister. Boy did we have a story to tell them!

"So, as you know, Mom is pregnant. We want to let you know that there is more than one baby."

"There's two!" our six-year-old daughter Mia shouted.

"Well, you're getting warmer..." Savanna intoned.

"Mom! There's three?" Bo, our eight-year-old questioned loudly. We explained to the kids that the Doctor saw three babies, but we could only hear two heartbeats. Bo immediately responded, "We have to pray for that third baby!"

If anyone knew how to throw a reality punch, it was Bo. He's a sensitive kid, much more mature than a typical kid his age. I had been thinking to myself, *Two babies is doable, but three babies requires a true zone defense*. But Bo put those thoughts into perspective. Baby C was there and, as soon as Bo spoke, I immediately became committed to that baby. An actual human being who required our full attention and commitment as parents.

We all began rooting for Baby C.

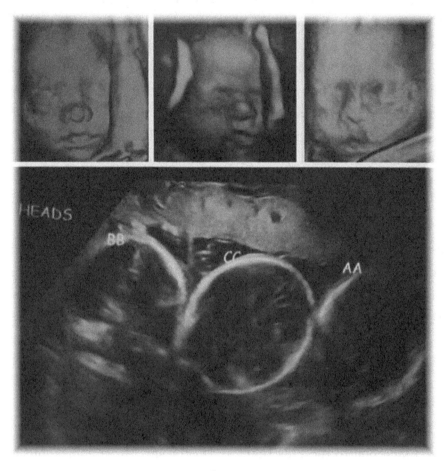

An ultrasound picture of the triplets.

2
PANIC ATTACK

Two weeks later, we found ourselves walking down the hall to receive the news about Baby C. He was one of us, and we all had accepted him as part of the family. But, as the doctor warned, there was a significant chance we wouldn't hear a heartbeat. We had also prepared ourselves for that possibility.

The doctor began the ultrasound as we followed along with her on the screen. We saw Baby A, listened to the heartbeat. She moved the wand to Baby B and we heard the simultaneous heartbeat. We were anxious as she moved the wand over the shadow toward Baby C. She adjusted the machine volume. There was nothing. She maneuvered the wand back and forth, and angled it differently than the other babies. She made a few changes on the machine and the pressure began to mount. My heartbeat was fast. I knew that whatever results we got that day were out of my control. As people often say, "Whatever happens is supposed to happen." I was okay with that.

Then suddenly the machine picked up a noise, a subtle but strong heartbeat, one that appeared louder and stronger than the other two babies. "Congratulations," the doctor said, "You are having triplets."

We were officially "Tate, party of eight!" I've never been opposed to a big family. Being Mormons in Utah, six kids is not out of the norm. But it was out of the norm for me because I have always been a planner. I mean, it's my livelihood as a financial planner. That's what I do. I plan for my life, so I had planned on having four kids.

When I was team captain at the U of U, I thrived in pressure situations. There hadn't been many things in my life up, until this point, that got me flustered or sent me into a panic. But I had met my match. Even before we left the doctor's office, the thought of having three babies to care for was setting me over the edge.

We came home and told the kids that Baby C was alive and well. They were thrilled. I mean, why wouldn't they be? Each of them was gonna get a baby. I felt like we were Oprah handing out babies: "You get a baby, and you get a baby, and you get a baby. The entire audience gets a baby!" Everyone was thrilled at the thought of raising these babies, except for me. I was panicking. My mind was filled with all the expenses. How the hell was I going to pay for diapers, formula, clothes, and on and on? It was too early to determine the genders of the babies, but I was already thinking about wedding costs, tuition costs, insurance premiums. You name it, I was thinking it. I looked at the ultrasound shadows and I saw dollar signs.

The thought of family vacations, or lack thereof, really got me. That night I saw an ad on television for Disneyland and it was game over for me. I began sweating, I lost feeling in my hands (which happens a lot through the course of this book), my tongue began to tingle, and my lips became numb. I couldn't think about anything else. "Savanna! We are never going to Disneyland." I exclaimed. "Our kids will never know what it's like to experience the happiest place on earth." I was breathing quickly. Disneyland was the ultimate shot to the head. I didn't sleep that night.

I didn't have the courage to tell anyone that we were expecting triplets. I was in denial. Maybe it's called shock, but I didn't want to talk about it or tell anyone. I actually wanted to curl up in the fetal position and cry, all pride gone. So I kept it a secret, especially from my family.

But I knew that triplets would require commitment from everyone. We were not going to be able to do it alone, so after a few weeks I found the courage to tell my family and close friends. I remember going to lunch with two friends in the neighborhood. One had twins. I sat there, trying to engage in conversation with them, but nothing they said mattered to me. I was thinking about how I was going to tell them we were expecting three babies. That's not something that naturally comes up in conversation. I mean, what was I supposed to say, "Went to the doctor the other day and she informed us we were having three babies. How was your week?" It's not exactly a natural talking point.

I somehow diverted the conversation and got the guts to tell them. I was dreading their reaction. It may come as a surprise to you that males aren't the most supportive among the genders. Our way of showing support is making fun of each other. We pretty much live our lives like a universal locker room. We give each other crap. It's in our DNA. So I was cringing with my eyes slightly closed, waiting for the wisecrack.

"That's awesome man!" he said in a surprisingly energetic fashion. I was amazed.

"Awesome? How is that awesome?"

"Dude, you're gonna have your own sports team!" he said smiling back with his hands in the air as if he had just solved some sort of master puzzle. I couldn't help but smile at his energy. It was exactly what I needed to hear. Of course it took something sports related to get me excited for these babies.

There are phases that you go through when you find out you are having triplets. There's the denial phase, which lasted for about six months. I obviously understood the facts, but it still didn't seem real to me. Then, there is the preparation phase. This is like a honeymoon period for people expecting babies. You probably know exactly what I am talking about. It's the phase when you are searching for cute newborn clothes, shoes, cribs, strollers, and so on. This is the time you start researching names and meanings of names and share every ultrasound picture with anyone and everyone you know, even people you don't know. Expecting a baby is euphoric and special, so why not? It should be exciting.

This is something that we had already experienced, three times over. This time, we were experiencing the preparation phase but it didn't have the same euphoric feel to me. I don't know why, maybe it was because we were doing everything times three. That meant three cribs, three wardrobes, three changing tables, three high chairs—I could keep going but you get the picture. Buying those things are fun, but buying those things three times over is torture. It physically hurt me. I would sweat when I looked at the amount of money we were spending.

Oh yeah, and we had to purchase a new car. Just a minor detail. I had very little pride left in me, but whatever pride remained wasn't allowing me to get a van. Especially not one of those fifteen-passenger behemoths. That was a deal breaker. You might as well turn in your man card if you purchase one of those things. I settled for a Chevy Suburban. Although not the most practical car in the world, it preserved some of the pride still left in this Dad bod.

Although expensive, the preparation phase was good for me because it gave me things to do. It kept my mind occupied, because I was extremely worried that I was going to have three girls. Don't get me wrong, I love my daughters but three of them going through junior-high drama would put me into a mental institution.

We were excited to find out the genders. When the doctor moved the wand over Baby A, she announced, "It's a girl." The pressure was on! *What would I actually do if I had triplet daughters?* I thought to myself. I truly believed God was going to give me all girls. I felt it was some sort of lesson I needed to learn, perhaps patience. But I began thinking over all the characteristics that I lacked as a father of soon-to-be triplet daughters. I felt the beads of sweat piling on my palms as I waited to hear the gender of Baby B.

"It's a boy." I exhaled deeply, clinching my fist as if I had just won the lottery. I had never felt so much relief in my life. I had been a part of some incredible accomplishments during my sports career, but this one topped them all.

I didn't even care what gender Baby C was at this point. It didn't matter. I knew that it wasn't three girls, so anything other than that was a bonus. The sweat was gone and I felt relieved as I waited for it. "And Baby C is a boy," she said. *Two boys I can throw the ball with,* I thought as I daydreamed about some future pick-up games in the backyard. Life was good!

Names came next. We had always loved the name Reese, so Baby A, our little girl, became Reese. We were drawn to the name Heath. It was a strong, solid name that could be given to a person with confidence. That was it, we decided Baby B was Heath. We wanted a name that correlated with Heath and we liked the idea of having the same letters for both the boys. Admittedly, it's a bit cliché, but because people would recognize them as a package, we felt a need to have two names that would roll off the tongue when we said them together. We came across the name Hayes and loved it immediately. It rolled off the tongue the way we wanted it to and included the same qualities. It was powerful and manly. It was a name that wasn't common and was memorable. Baby C became Hayes.

The cribs were purchased, the names were picked out. Their rooms were made and decorated, and the Suburban was purchased.

My wallet was dented and the expenses were high, but the preparation phase was almost complete. All we lacked now were the babies, the actual human beings. Bring on the babies!

3

BABIES ARE BORN

_W_eek thirty-four is the magical time when triplets need to come out. That was when our championship game was scheduled. And we were on track to make it. Savanna's health throughout the pregnancy was unbelievably good. Oddly enough, she seemed to handle this pregnancy better than the previous ones, and she was being a true champ. Then it happened.

We had just finished our thirty-one week appointment and things looked great. The doctor was pleased with how things were progressing: the babies' heartbeats were strong and all three were healthy. We left that appointment excited that everything was on track for a healthy caesarean in three weeks.

Savanna had a routine stress test scheduled a few hours later, and she went to the appointment while I went back to the office. I know, I probably sound like a terrible husband, but give me a break. I had just been with her hours before and the doctor told us everything looked amazing. How was I supposed to know she would go into labor? But she did.

The nurses had connected all the wires to Savanna's belly and only a few minutes into the stress test the nurse began to notice the labor-like contractions. Of course, Savanna didn't feel them, being the toughest human being I have ever met. I've never seen or heard her complain of pain. She puts me to shame.

I received a text from her that said, "Apparently I'm having contractions every two minutes so they are sending me to labor and delivery." The limitation of texting is that you can't get a feel for the tone behind the message. It appeared extremely casual, which is just like Savanna. She is the most easy-going person in the world and nothing seems to get her to panic. We balance each other out nicely that way. She is always optimistic and never dramatic. I'm the more emotional one. Things get to me.

I immediately replied, "Wait, you are having contractions? Are you going into labor? Should I come over?" I sat at my desk, nervously waiting for her reply.

"I don't think it's a big deal, I wouldn't worry about it," she messaged back. I did the math on the contractions and began to understand it was more than just some cramps. I knew it was serious. I immediately dropped what I was doing at the office and hurried to the hospital. The babies were coming and there was nothing we could do to stop it. Game on.

There was a drill that my head coach, Urban Meyer, would make us do that required us to compete under pressure. We called it "the circle drill." The entire team made a circle as Urban chose two players at random to come into the circle and drive each other out of it. The experience was horrible. You were forced to compete against one of your teammates in front of your peers and coaches, knowing that one person was going to succeed and one was going to fail. I despised that drill. Every time Urban blew the whistle and yelled "circle drill!," I was immediately overwhelmed by extreme anxiety. I would try to blend in with the team and avoid eye contact with him, for fear he would call my name.

The very thought of the drill made me quiver. But the drill paled in comparison to the pressure I experienced as I drove to the hospital. I was about to add three babies to my life, making that six freaking kids. That's a lot, even for Mormons.

The doctors wanted to do an emergency C-section. There was an entire team of physicians in the room—I guess they don't slack with triplets. Just after midnight on March 12, 2015 the Tate triplets were born. Baby A, Reese Avi Tate, was the first one born at three pounds, eight ounces. They immediately took Reese to the room next door to clean her up and clear out her lungs, the standard protocol stuff. A few minutes later they delivered Heath Tillman Tate. He was the chubby one of the bunch, weighing a whopping three pounds, fourteen ounces. The physicians seemed a little more concerned about him at delivery. He experienced the most shock coming into this world, and was immediately placed on a ventilator. We waited a few more minutes, and then they delivered our sweet Baby C, Hayes Kyle Tate, weighing in at three pounds, eleven ounces. As with the previous two babies, they took Hayes, cleaned him up, and did the usual examination before placing him in a blanket close to his brother and sister.

I stood there in complete disbelief, motionless. I felt inadequate in that moment as I wondered, *How am I supposed to provide enough love to all of these babies?* I felt this the entire time I was in the room. The doctors tended to Savanna while I met each of them.

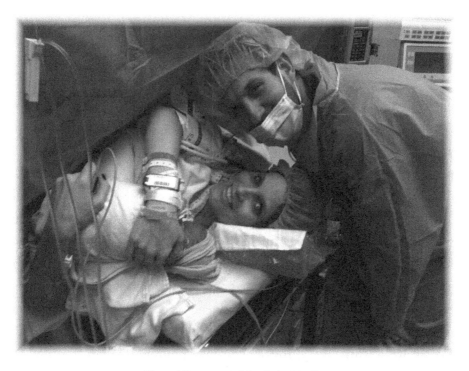

Me and Savanna holding baby Heath.

I first walked over to Reese. She was so tiny, almost doll-like with her strands of black hair and dark eyebrows. I felt awkward kissing her because I wasn't used to a baby so small. In fact, we were known to make exceptionally large babies. Bo, our oldest, had weighed exactly ten pounds at birth. He was the ultimate trophy baby for someone like me, as I was a sophomore in college, still playing football, when he was born. I bragged to all my teammates that I produced a defensive lineman.

I then walked over to Heath. Although only six ounces heavier than Reese, he was a lot huskier. A condensed version of Bo, with a bulldog appearance to him. His eyebrows scowled while they continued to work on clearing his little lungs. I was hesitant to touch Heath, with all the machines that were connected to him, including a ventilator. Still, I leaned over, kissed him, and introduced myself.

Hayes was only a few feet away and I leaned over his little crib to peer into his tiny eyes. "Can I hold?" I asked hesitantly, not sure of the protocols. A nurse bundled his little body in a warm hospital blanket and put a beanie over his dirty-blonde hair. I grabbed him, cradled him in my arms in classic newborn fashion, and began examining his entire body. I went through the classic dad checklist, making sure he had all his toes and fingers. He was perfect. All three were perfect, with thirty fingers and thirty toes.

I was still in shock, doing my best to not pass out from the overwhelming feelings of stress and inadequacy. I have never passed out in my life, but if there was ever any opportunity for a first, now was the time. I made my way around the baby incubators, trying to spend an equal amount of time with each of them. I would feel guilty if I spent too much time with one and not the others. I even tracked the amount of time on my watch to ensure no favoritism.

After only a few hours with them on earth, I was already finding time distribution difficult as I thought, *How am I going to do this?* This was only half of my kids. Three older children needed the same amount of love and attention.

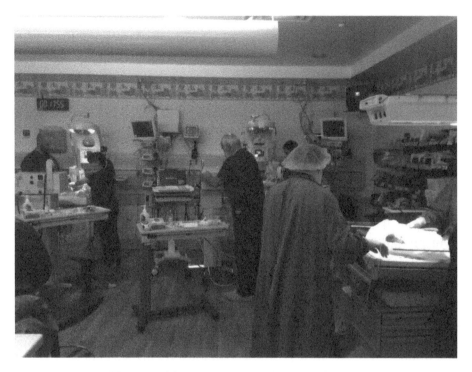

The team of doctors and nurses attending the triplets.

For the most part, the babies were healthy, they just needed a few machines and chords attached to their teeny bodies. Heath was on a ventilator for the first week or so. He was the fat and happy one of the bunch, and it was as if he liked having something else breathe for him while he was laying around in the crib all day. I couldn't help but think of that little mouse from *Cinderella*, Gus. Reese needed a little assistance breathing for only a day, since girls are usually more resilient. Actually, girls are tougher period. I would never want to mess with Savanna, and there was little doubt that Reese was taking after her mom. Then there was Hayes. He was only on a ventilator for a few hours, immediately after birth. The physicians were amazed with his resiliency and toughness. Typically the baby delivered last goes through the most shock and struggles with living fundamentals, like eating and breathing. But not Hayes, he was different. Hayes thrived from the moment they took him from the womb. He had a toughness to him, both mentally and physically. He never seemed to cry when they poked him with needles or pried him with the various hospital devices. He had an extremely high threshold for pain tolerance. I was amazed at his ability to thrive at every major developmental stage. Whether it was getting off the ventilator, latching on to a bottle, or going home, Hayes always led the pack. He was definitely showing up his older chubby brother and petite sister.

Because it was cold season, the nurses wouldn't let the babies' older siblings into the room. But they could meet each other through a window. As I walked into the hospital with the kids, they couldn't control their excitement. They giggled as they scurried down the hall, ready to meet the babies who would soon change their lives. The meeting was brief, and it was special. With the help of two other nurses, Savanna opened the blinds and held the babies up to the window for the kids to see them. The kiddos were overcome with joy, full-on Christmas-morning joy.

"Bo, Mia, Wes, meet your triplet brothers and sister," I said to them. They laughed and giggled and made some classic, childlike comments that were as insensitive and inappropriate as kids typically do. It felt right seeing all six of them together that afternoon. It didn't necessarily make sense, but our circus-like family felt complete somehow. The love was palpable and, for whatever reason, that moment brought me a sense of calmness and reassurance that everything was going to fall into place. Don't be fooled, I was still an emotional wreck and the paranoia of inadequacy still consumed my every thought, but that moment brought a sense of happiness and completion to our family.

The babies were progressing developmentally, with Hayes still leading the pack. He was meeting every requirement. He was a newborn all-star: sucking as he should, breathing with no assistance, and gaining weight much more rapidly than the other babies. He adjusted to life after the womb seamlessly. In fact, doctors were so pleased with his progression that they let us take him home, while the other two stayed at the hospital. They hadn't quite met their developmental stages, but Hayes was coming home.

I was so proud of Hayes for being the first one home. Maybe it's because the doctors warned us during the night of their birth that the last one born usually develops much more slowly. I felt like Hayes was an underdog, if you will. I saw a bit of me in him. I always felt like it was me against the world when it came to my sports career. I was always "too small" or "too slow" by those on the outside. I'm not exactly physically imposing. If you saw me, you would never think I was an all-conference football player; tennis maybe, but not football. I was athletic and played both offense and defense in high school. I excelled in college at safety, mostly because I learned to do things most players hated doing, like tackling and blitzing. Playing safety was a dirty job, a tough guy's duty, and it required a "chip-on-the-shoulder" mentality. I knew that for me to succeed at a school like the University of Utah, I needed to be the best tackler on the team. So I did just that. I led the team in tackles both my junior and senior years. I prided myself on being strong and physical. Yes, I was undersized compared to the players I faced, but I had some nasty to me on the football field. Because I always had to prove the critics wrong.

Hayes was taking that same role as the underdog, and he was thriving. He was tough. I felt extremely connected to him. In just forty days on earth, I could tell we were similar. He was my boy and I already took so much pride in him.

Then Reese came home to join us, followed by our chubby guy, Heath. Finally, after forty-seven days in the hospital, the triplets were all home and all eight of us were finally together under one roof. I couldn't help but think of the Diddy song "Coming Home." I don't necessarily enjoy his music, but those lyrics were on repeat in my brain.

Me holding the triplets together for the first time.

4

STICK TO THE SCHEDULE

During the preparation phase of the pregnancy, Savanna and I turned to every source of support we could find, hoping to find the right system for managing three babies. We needed to be efficient with our time because we had three other children to care for also. Social media helped, whether it was Instagram or Facebook. We culled advice from people who had been in our shoes, or were currently in our same situation. Savanna joined a triplet support site, where she could connect with women all over the world. The consensus theme was "stick to a schedule." That was touted as the only way we would survive these next two years of our lives.

It was excellent advice, but it scared the crap out of me. You see, Savanna and schedules don't work. She's never been on time for anything in her life, she was even late to our wedding. Don't get me wrong. I am lucky she even showed up to marry me so I'm willing to forgive her for being late, but that is Savanna. She's not a scheduler. Time is just an arbitrary number to her. I, on the other hand, am nothing short of a drill sergeant when it comes to schedules and managing time. Coach Kyle Whittingham had a saying he would repeat to our team often: "If you are early, you are on time. If you are on time, you are late. And if you are late, don't bother showing up." I hated being late for anything. My entire life ran on a schedule, and I didn't even need a watch. My brain was trained to determine when to wake up, when to eat, when to sleep, when to go to the office, when to take the kids to their activities. I could "stick to the schedule." That was right up my alley.

After a lot of trial and error, with many sleepless nights and zombie days, we figured out the secret, triplet algorithm for success. It was incredible. We alternated the feeding schedule so that Savanna would feed the babies at 9 p.m. before heading to bed. I would then take over the midnight shift and stay up feeding, changing, and burping the babies before they fell asleep. Savanna would then take over, and wake up for a 3 a.m. feeding session as I slept. This meant we both got almost six hours of uninterrupted sleep. I felt like we deserved some sort of award for figuring this out.

The feedings continued to be tag-teamed throughout the first nine months of their lives. At one point, Savanna and I turned the feeding sessions into a game or competition. We would wager bets on the amount of diapers we were going to change in one session, or how fast we could finish burping, feeding, and changing them before putting them back down for bed. I still own the record on diapers changed in one feeding session: ten diapers. Yes, ten diapers in a span of forty-five minutes.

Those feeding sessions were stressful. I would sweat profusely in that room. I had been part of some excruciating workouts during my football days, especially with Coach Urban Meyer. In some ways, I should thank him for teaching me how to perform under pressure, both mentally and physically, with only a few hours of sleep. I would sometimes record these feeding sessions on my phone and share them with our followers on Instagram and Facebook. I wanted to give people a glimpse of what was going on in the "Tate Family Circus Show."

Overall, we had our system down. We ran by the schedule and we were efficient. The other kids were helpful too. They loved coming home from school and grabbing one of the babies. They took turns with each baby and passed them around to make sure that each of them spent quality time with all three. They wanted to make sure they didn't play favorites, except for Wes, who was three years old at the time, he had his favorite.

"Dad" he said in his small little voice "I like all the babies, but Hayes is my favorite." I couldn't help but laugh. Wes quickly developed an inseparable bond with Hayes, and Hayes loved him. Wes always made Hayes smile and laugh. Any time that Wes entered the room, Hayes would laugh or smile. Wes was the Will Ferrell of siblings in Hayes's eyes, the ultimate comedian. It was really good to see Wes bond with one of the babies, since he had just been replaced in the pecking order, from youngest to middle of the pack.

Throughout the entire first year, we were sticking to our schedule and very few things got in the way. We had so many people willing to help with the babies. But oddly enough, we didn't need much help with the juggling act. We were managing extremely well with the system we had in place. I was CEO of this baby factory and those three tiny humans knew I meant business. I became a newborn feeding specialist. Each night I hurried in, changed their diapers and propped the bottles on pillows as I sat back and caught up on my social media, sometimes even enjoying a refreshing Coke Zero. I even posted videos and pictures from time to time, documenting the controlled chaos in that room. Those moments were surprisingly peaceful, much different than the first month or so, when I left the room with a soaked T-shirt from the amount of sweat I had accumulated.

Savanna and I have always had an uncanny way of adapting to each chapter of our lives together. And this "triplet chapter" was no different. We were finding so much joy in our life with the triplets. Every night after the 9 p.m. feeding session, as the babies peacefully slept, we would find ourselves in their rooms staring in amazement at the creations we had made.

We would first go into the boy's room and check on Heath, our "chubby guy," curled up with his bum in the air, probably dreaming of food. Then we would make our way over to Hayes. He would be lying on his right side with a slight grin on his face. Hayes was always smiling, even in his sleep. If Heath was dreaming of the next meal, Hayes was dreaming of Heaven and angels. There always seemed to be something joyful and wise going on inside Hayes's head that we couldn't put a finger on, but it intrigued us. We would then make our way across the hall to check on our little Reese. She was always a mess when she slept. Her position changed each time we checked on her, often sticking a foot out between the crib railings. Her dark little hair was always all over the place.

These babies were a blessing to our family, an absolute present from Heaven.

All three babies lined up on the couch after an afternoon feeding session.

5

THIS ISN'T SO BAD

July marked the beginning of a new era. We were living with triplets. People would always ask us, "Isn't it just the worst to take care of three babies?" Their facial expressions begged for a certain "life sucks" reply. We shocked them by responding that it was actually incredibly fun and rewarding. Judging by their reaction, they didn't believe us. I know it doesn't make sense, but it was fun. It was so much more enjoyable and entertaining than I had ever imagined. Life was incredible.

"How lucky are we?" I would frequently say to Savanna before she dozed off to sleep. We were finding so much joy in raising these three little humans.

Our new chapter was filled with so many laughable moments as we watched the babies develop. We witnessed every new task they learned. We watched Heath and Hayes as they had their first fight. They were on the floor, and Heath was playing with a ball that had holes he could stick his fat, little fingers through. Hayes became intrigued with the toy and reached over to take the ball from Heath. He tugged with all his might. Heath was curious about this opposition and pulled back. The two began a tug-of-war, their first brotherly fight. We immediately got our phones and started recording this adorable moment.

Heath and Hayes swaddled in a blanket.

Heath had the strength, but Hayes had the fight. They tugged back and forth several times before Heath began to cry. Hayes peered at his older brother with a smirk on his face. It was as if he was thinking, *What's this guy's problem? Toughen up, dude, you outweigh me by almost three pounds.* They continued for several minutes, with each of them winning at some point, before we finally got Hayes his own toy to play with. Heath's face was red and his eyes were filled with crocodile tears. Hayes, on the other hand, was calm. He had a stoic look, with nothing but determination in his eyes. Nothing could faze our little Hayes. It was a moment that absolutely reflected the personalities of our two baby boys. I, of course, wondered what their first football practice together would be like.

As football season came to an end, the weather changed from crispy fall afternoons to winter days filled with snowflakes. Life was becoming extremely busy, packed to the brim with holiday activities. From the outside looking in, it was complete chaos, but to us it was fun. Each one of us was finding extreme pleasure with the business of this new life. The older kids loved watching their baby brothers and sister learn new things. The babies were our family's entertainment. Now almost nine months old, they were developing as usual. All three babies were sitting up, and two were rolling over. Hayes was the first to do both. He was the overachiever, and I was sure the other two babies would soon grow envious of him because they were always following his lead. We were still keeping the babies on a regular schedule, but as naps became less frequent, we needed more ways to entertain them. We spent waking hours rotating different toys between all three of them to keep their attention. They were learning, progressing, and having fun. There was really nothing stressing us out those winter days, other than usual holiday chaos with Christmas right around the corner.

Christmas is always stressful when you come from large families, as Savanna and I both do. There are expectations from both families, and that didn't change despite the fact that we were hauling three babies around. We tried using the "triplet card" to escape some of the less meaningful events, but it never seemed to work. People still wanted to see us at parties. So it seemed like every day in December was filled with nonstop activities and events. We were constantly loading up the car in the freezing cold to see the grandparents, aunts, uncles, and cousins. I'm not sure if it's a Mormon thing, but each family seems to have six Christmas parties in addition to the actual Christmas Eve and Day.

Around the fifteenth of December, the babies were getting sick. They all had typical runny noses and earaches, as they were grabbing their ears throughout the day. The good thing about having triplets is that you know if one baby is sick, all of them are sick. Hayes was sleepier than his brother and sister, which continued for a week or two. He was lethargic and often needed an extra nap just to keep his energy up. This threw off the typical schedule, but we were now comfortable so we could give each baby what was needed. But then his energy level became so low that he had no desire to roll over or sit up anymore.

"Hayes's sickness must've hit him harder than Reese and Heath," I said to Savanna. She agreed. We took him to the pediatrician, who looked in his ears and noticed an ear infection.

"It's probably just a virus and it's taking him longer to get over it," the pediatrician said, reassuring us that it wasn't anything major. It was a moment of relief, as we had feared something more serious. We took him home and gave him time to recover from the virus, as the doctor advised. Every morning for a week we would wake up, hurry to Hayes's room to see if his energy had picked up, only to be disappointed.

Hayes was always so smiley and social in the mornings, and we craved that same interaction while he was sick. We could tell he didn't feel well at all. He was the first thing on my mind when I woke up, and the last thing I pondered when I went to bed. He wasn't getting any better and we both felt something serious was going on. But Savanna was doing her best to stay calm to prevent setting me off into a panic.

"It's not a virus." I often told Savanna throughout the day as we texted back and forth. She tried to calm me, like she always does.

"The doctor reassured us that he has a virus," she said in a calming, confident manner. But Savanna was worried as well and I could sense it. On New Year's Eve, Savanna left me with the babies while she took the kids to her sister's house. I sat and observed

Hayes for most of the day. I was supposed to be watching all three babies, but I admit that I wasn't. My entire focus was on Hayes. I watched as he struggled to lift his head. The other babies were rolling around and engaging with the toys I had set out for them, but not Hayes. He had zero interest. His energy level was extremely low. So low that he couldn't even turn his head to observe his triplet brother and sister. I observed him for a few hours before finally lying him down for a much-needed nap. As I did, he fell instantaneously asleep.

My stomach sank and my eyes teared up. I grabbed my phone and sent Savanna a text, "Babe, something is going on with Hayes." I later found out that Savanna was relaying this same concern to her sister just as I texted her. "I'm scared," I continued. "I think there is something major going on." I was wiping tears from my eyes so I could read her reply.

A few minutes later she responded: "Okay, let's take him to the ER."

She wasn't trying to stay strong, she wasn't trying to calm me down, and there were no reassurances. I sat there in a panic while I waited for her to get home, with tears now rolling down my cheeks.

Hayes in his favorite recliner chair.

6

TRUSTING OUR INSTINCTS

---

*I*f there is anything I have learned throughout this entire journey, it's that parents know what is going on with their children better than any expert. We know our children's habits, we know their personalities, and we know when things don't seem right. Every parent I have ever met shares this same quality. It's one of the things we are blessed with, and entitled to, as caregivers. Savanna and I have been blessed when it comes to good instincts, and we let them guide us, whether they come naturally or from God. And our instincts were kicking in. Hayes was sick.

That New Year's Eve, Savanna arrived home and we loaded Hayes in the back of the Suburban for the short drive to the hospital. My initial thought was to take him to a top children's hospital, but our insurance didn't cover it. We walked into the waiting room with Hayes. It was crowded and relatively noisy. After twenty minutes or so, a nurse came and escorted us to the next available room. Visiting the Doctor was never an enjoyable experience, but I felt like we were going to finally be guided about what to do so Hayes could get better. Earlier that day, I had done some Internet research on his symptoms. I searched for anything I could find about lack of energy. But Hayes didn't have a fever, and every article that I read included some sort of fever as one of the primary symptoms. This made things extremely difficult to diagnose.

A doctor came in, asked the basic questions, and examined our little nine-month-old boy. They took a blood sample, and one of the specialists recognized us. "You are the Tate triplets!" she said in amazement, "I follow your family on Instagram." We felt flattered, but now wasn't the time for small talk. We waited anxiously in that ER room for the blood tests to come back. Hayes was comfortable in Savanna's arms as he started nodding off. The doctor came back and began getting additional information on Hayes and his condition.

"He's been extremely lethargic," we said as Hayes lounged in Savanna's arm. "He is a triplet so we have noticed his lack of energy compared to his brother and sister. We've also noticed that he doesn't have much of an appetite."

"Has he had any fevers?" the doctor asked.

"No," I replied. "He hasn't had any fevers, but he has an ear infection. His triplet brother and sister had the same ear infections a few weeks ago, but they are doing fine now. Hayes hasn't seemed to recover."

"Has he been throwing up?"

"No, he hasn't thrown up," Savanna responded. At this point, the doubts began. *Are we those crazy parents?* I thought to myself. We all know *those* parents who are overly protective, obsessive, and concerned, who freak out if their kid falls down and gets a scrape. We have never been *those* parents. If anything, we are the opposite, telling the kids to toughen up when they fall down. I felt a little odd as the doctor continued to ask questions. I even began doubting myself during the entire examination: *He's not throwing up. He doesn't have a fever. Why am I here?* I'm sure we may have even sounded a little crazy to the Doctor when the only symptom we could muster was his lethargy.

As those thoughts were running back and forth through my head, Hayes threw up—for the first time since symptoms began a couple weeks before. We had just given him a bottle to help relax him in the hospital room and out it came, all over Savanna's lap. In some really odd way, it was actually a relief to us. I'm pretty sure it was a relief to Hayes, judging by the amount of vomit that came out his mouth. It basically told the doctor that Hayes wasn't feeling well, and that there was more to his sickness than just "lack of energy."

As we were cleaning up, the bloodwork came back abnormal. The doctor proceeded to tell me some medical terminology for "virus," as it appeared that Hayes had one. We left the hospital a bit more relieved than we had arrived because the vomiting seemed to confirm the diagnosis. Our minds were eased for a few hours, which felt wonderful considering we had been worrying day and night more than two weeks.

We monitored him closely that night and into the next day. He threw up the following morning and again that afternoon. Whatever relief we felt the night before disappeared. The worries settled in again. Our instincts kept pushing us for further tests or opinions. I searched day and night on Google and WebMD. Something was telling me and Savanna that this wasn't the virus that the doctor had described to us. I felt prompted to search for the signs of meningitis. I knew that throwing up and lack of energy were two primary symptoms of meningitis, so I put those symptoms into the search engine. The list of symptoms read: throwing up, lethargic, fever, rash, and swollen fontanel. I showed Savanna the screen and we googled the definition of "fontanel," which is also known as a baby's soft spot.

Hayes was asleep along with the other babies, but I wasted no time as I ran to his room. Savanna continued reading the symptoms. I pushed open the door and rushed to Hayes's crib. I grabbed his tiny head and felt his soft spot. It was a little raised, but it wasn't as if I had a lot of experience in this arena. Fortunately for us, we had two other babies to use as comparison. I turned to my left and grabbed Heath's head. I felt around with my fingers and closely examined with my eyes. It felt a little different to me, but I needed further proof. I hurried across the hall to Reese's room, who woke with the sound of the door. I kissed her on the cheek to calm her down and grabbed her little head and examined it closely. I moved her dark brown hair side to side to get a better look.

My heart skipped a beat and the blood rushed from my face. I closed her door behind me and crossed the hall again to the boys' room. I cupped Hayes's head again and immediately knew. His fontanel was raised.

I turned off the light and went to the top of the stairs. "Savanna," I yelled down, in a panicked manner, "his soft spot is raised." She hurried up and examined for herself. She felt it too.

"What do we do?" we asked ourselves. It was if we were solving some sort of crime-scene investigation. In some way, we were. Our instincts were pushing us closer to an explanation. We simply didn't believe that he had a virus.

The following morning, we scheduled an appointment to see the pediatrician. The doctor came in, did an examination of Hayes, and asked the basic questions. Savanna was armed for this appointment. She had taken a video of Hayes in his exercise saucer compared to his brother and sister, a video that demonstrated his lethargy. He was motionless, hardly able to lift his little head. Savanna also played a video of Hayes from the month prior, for comparison. The doctor blew it off.

"This means nothing to me," she said encouraging Savanna to put her phone away. It was as if she was put off by the whole visit. "That video tells me nothing."

We felt like crazy, paranoid parents all over again. There was no sense of urgency on the doctor's part—we were obviously just the next appointment scheduled on her calendar. She was ready to bill our insurance and move on to the next patient. She ordered some lab tests and sent us on our way.

"We will call you if the labs results show any abnormalities," she said as she hurried us out the door. "It's apparent that he has a virus and it's taking him an extremely long time to get over it." Those were her final words as she walked us down the hall, and they were extremely discouraging. I was mad: *It isn't a virus!* I felt hopeless.

I have two other babies for comparison and one of them is not like the others, I thought as I planned the next path to take for additional answers and opinions. At home, the anger grew. Anger is an emotion that drives me. I don't turn green like the Incredible Hulk, but it brings out an unparalleled level of determination. Very little can get in my way. Focus settles in and my mind becomes unwavering. I was going to get to the bottom of Hayes's illness and there was absolutely nothing that could get in my way. I picked up the phone, ready to challenge the doctor. I had a list of items to discuss with her and I wanted accurate assessments. I wanted her definition of a "virus." My instincts were telling me she was full of it. She was treating us like a routine part of her job.

"Give me the doctor please," I said to the nurse, in a confident yet demanding tone. When the doctor answered, she sounded ticked off. I wondered if that was just her personality, and if so, she definitely shouldn't practice medicine. Then I began my angry-Steve interrogation.

I described Hayes as a triplet who has so far shared symptoms with his brother and sister. But this time, the others aren't sick. "Please explain to me why this is the exception," I said, waiting for her response.

"The other two babies have nothing to do with Hayes. I have seen multiples before, each with their independent sicknesses," she said impatiently. I accepted her response and moved on.

"What about his raised soft spot?" I asked her.

"I examined his raised soft spot and it appeared to be normal," she replied quickly.

"Normal? It's raised!" I stated firmly and loudly. "His soft spot is raised compared to his brother and sister."

"His soft spot was soft, not hard. So there is no room for concern on my end," she said before continuing with her opinion. "Your son has a virus and he is dehydrated." That response solidified my unimpressed impression of her. It was an amateur answer, straight from the memory bank. The doctor was sticking with the script; her answer rolled off her tongue as if she used it repeatedly with all the parents who had seen her that day. I decided to call her bluff.

"A raised soft spot is not a sign of dehydration. In fact, it's the exact opposite. If he was dehydrated then he would have a sunken soft spot," I said, matter of factly. "Everything that I have read about raised soft spots advises immediate medical attention." The anger built as I finished my thought.

"If I was really worried about your son's soft spot I would've sent you to the ER," she replied. "He has a virus. I advise you to stay off the Internet and quit googling. It only makes you a paranoid parent," she said. My blood began to boil, which she must have known would happen because she quickly added, "I have other patients waiting for me, but I appreciate the phone call. Goodbye." She hung up before I could say anything else.

I punched my desk. The rage was that uncontrollable. Nobody seemed to be taking us seriously. *My son is sick and it's not a freaking virus,* I thought as I gave my desk another swift punch. I tried to hold back the tears of hopelessness, but I couldn't. I sat there crying with my head in my hands.

The frustration grew and feeling of hopelessness continued throughout the night and into the next morning. It was January 7th. Hayes woke up with the same lethargy, but he hadn't thrown up. We were thrilled. We naively felt a sense of hope that perhaps this "virus" was passing. We got him up, took him downstairs, and placed him in his favorite rocker chair. I ran to the basement to grab Hayes's favorite puppet, determined to make him laugh. One of a dad's required duties is making the children laugh. Laughter solves everything. *Maybe he needs a reason to feel better,* I thought as I searched for the puppet. Hayes had a laugh that could make things better—it filled any room, and there was something inside of me that craved it. I needed to hear it for my soul.

As I was digging through a basket of toys, I heard the kids yell down: "Hayes threw up!" I stopped immediately. It was a kick to the gut, a punch to the face. I thought we were actually turning a corner. Boy, was I wrong.

That morning, I was extremely discouraged as I left the house to go to work, and my mind stayed focused on Hayes and nothing else. I wanted to head home to be with Savanna, but I had scheduled a lunch with a close friend, Mike Greene. I believe certain people have been put in my life for a reason. I know God has done that throughout this entire journey, and one of those people is Mike, a guy I had met a year before. His son was about the same age as Bo, and when I was putting together a football staff for a little league team, Mike agreed to coach with me. We quickly gelled. When it came to coaching, we were a little rough around the edges. But we both have emotional, sensitive sides when it comes to family. I respect Mike with all my heart.

Mike had lost a son, Jackson, to cancer a few years before I met him. I knew it was still hard on him. I could see it in his eyes when we coached together and I admired him for his strength. He's a guy that I really look up to.

We sat down at a table and I immediately began to vent about my concern for Hayes. I had yet to share with anyone other than Savanna, so it felt really good. I held back tears as I spoke. Mike was really the only person in the world who could totally empathize with me at that moment. And I could drop some major cuss words, knowing there would be no judgement from him. Most of my close friends are Mormons and have never used a foul word in their lives. I've been in a lot of locker rooms, so I can swear like the best of them. I only do it in special moments—and this was one of them.

As I sat there tossing the food around my plate, venting to Mike, my phone rang. I looked down and saw that it was Savanna. I almost didn't need to answer it, I knew what was going on.

"Hello?" I answered hesitantly. I knew it was about Hayes.

"Steve, we gotta go to the hospital now," she said. Her voice was trembling.

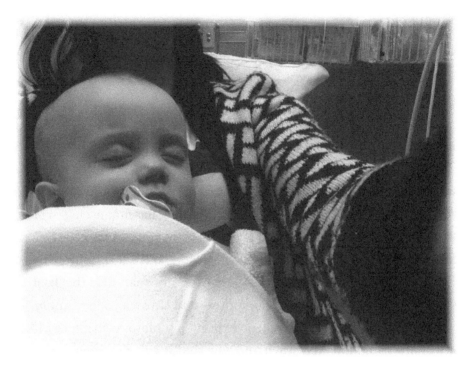

Savanna holding Hayes at one of our hospital visits.

7

THE DAY OUR LIVES CHANGED FOREVER

*T*here are some days that change your life forever. Every American remembers the details of where they were, and what they were doing, on September 11, 2001, when the World Trade Center towers went down. Every single detail gets scarred in your brain. January 7, 2016, was the same sort of day for me. It was a day that will forever be remembered, despite my wish to forget.

"I'll be right there," I said to Savanna and ended the call. Mike understood the severity of the situation and I took off immediately. I have no recall of whether I paid for the meal or not. I'm pretty sure I stiffed Mike and left him with the bill, but I know he didn't care. He could tell that things were about to get serious.

As I drove home, I called Savanna from the privacy of the car. "What's going on?"

"I just got off the phone with Rick," she said. Rick Bentley is my brother-in-law, a radiologist practicing at a hospital in Idaho Falls. "He told us that we need to go to the ER immediately." The panic in her voice was hard to hear, because it was so atypical for Savanna.

"What did he say?" I responded softly, anticipating concerning news.

"He's really concerned about the raised soft spot."

I stepped harder on the gas pedal. Panic was setting in as I felt color drain from my face. I made it home in record time. Savanna had already put Hayes in his carseat and as she turned to me I could see the tears in her eyes. Our neighbor scurried over to watch the other babies.

It was eerie to back out of the driveway and make our way to Primary Children's Hospital—a much different feeling from the previous three times we taken him to see doctors. There was silence, not a word was exchanged between Savanna and I the entire way. I'll never forget that car ride to the hospital. It was a cold January afternoon, and the leather seats were stiff and icy cold. The weather fit the type of day we were about to experience: completely gray, dark, and gloomy. It felt depressing and hopeless. It felt heavy.

I looked back at our sweet boy in his carseat. Hayes had a blanket over him, but I knew his extremities were cold and chapped. It was another symptom we had started noticing in the past two nights as we lathered him in lotion and placed socks over his feet. He was peering out the window. Those perfect blue eyes were filled with innocence, unaware of the events that would soon transpire. My eyes, I'm sure, were the exact opposite: filled with fear. As I observed Hayes through the rearview mirror, tears swelled. My paternal instincts were screaming during that fifteen-minute drive. The intuition I had been feeling for the past month was flooding my every thought. I couldn't escape the fear. Although Hayes was blissfully unaware, Savanna and I had no doubt that things were getting serious. I knew this car ride was one that I would never forget, and unfortunately, I was right.

We parked the Suburban and started the dreaded walk toward the ER entrance. Hayes was in Savanna's arms as I followed behind. We were given the typical ER forms to fill out. A nurse came and greeted us, asking about the reason for our visit. We avoided talking about his vomiting and lack of energy, for fear that she would think it was just a minor visit.

"His soft spot is swollen."

The nurse stopped in her tracks. She felt his cold feet and guided us through the ER doors to an available room. She wrapped Hayes in a warm hospital blanket as he sat on Savanna's lap. The doctor walked in, accompanied by a fellow from the University of Utah since Primary Children's Hospital is a teaching institution. They asked in-depth questions as they did their examination. They focused primarily on his head and eyes. The examination was thorough and their questions were sincere. As the doctor examined Hayes, we voiced our concerns to her and she listened to every single word that came out of our mouths. It was the polar opposite of our meeting with the family physician the previous day. It was as if she was listening to us as a parent and not a physician. She was compassionate and real; her concern for our son's well-being was obvious. She was treating Hayes as if he were her own son, and I could tell she was a mom.

"Can we get a CT scan?" I asked, surprising myself. I hadn't planned on asking for one, but it suddenly felt necessary and I knew I needed to be blunt with my request. Without hesitation, the doctor agreed to order an immediate CT scan.

Hayes then fell asleep. After about fifteen minutes had passed, something woke him up. He moaned loudly. It was a dull, achy moan, and the physician heard it but didn't say anything at the time. As she later told us, she had recognized it immediately as a neurological moan. Without a doubt, in that moment, she had known something was neurologically wrong with Hayes.

Then they took us back to imaging. We placed Hayes on the cold hospital bed and a machine enclosed his head. The room was covered in Utah Jazz basketball decals to ease children's minds. But nothing was easing my mind at the moment; it would take a lot more than some sports logos to ease the pain I experienced as I watched them strap Hayes's forehead to the bed. They needed to stabilize his little body in order to get an accurate image of his brain. We distracted him with toys as they started taking the images. His sweet, innocent little eyes peered up at us in confusion, and we tried to maintain a calm presence. Hayes couldn't talk, nor did he understand the words coming from our mouths, but we knew he understood body language and the tone of voice. I focused on being as calm as I could for Hayes. They finished the CT scan in only a few minutes and escorted us back to the hospital room.

We waited. It was a wait unlike anything I had experienced in my life. My heart was thumping out of my chest and my palms were sweating. My fingers even began to tingle like they had when we found out we were having triplets—the sign of complete panic. Although the symptoms were similar, this time it was life or death panic. I was facing a fear that no parent should ever experience. I dreaded the results of that CT scan. I watched the closed door intently, refusing to blink, because I knew that as soon as it opened a scary, unforeseeable future would begin.

The door opened. I saw the expression on the doctor's face and my heart sank.

"We have answers." Her tone was soft and compassionate. "I'm so sorry to tell you this. There is a mass in the fourth ventricle of his brain." She pulled up the image on a computer and showed us the screen. Savanna and I were no experts, but it didn't take eight years of medical school to recognize what was going on in that black and white image. There was a giant spherical mass taking up a third of Hayes's brain. My eyes were scarred. A part of me died that moment.

"No!" Savanna screamed. "No! My Baby..." Her voice shook in heart wrenching anguish. As she started shaking and grabbing her face, I tried my best to console her. That was my job as a father and husband. It's part of the code, but I can guarantee you that whoever wrote that code never experience what I was going through. I sobbed as I held her head against my chest. I couldn't hold back anything. My heart felt hollowed as I stared at Hayes, and in my disbelief I almost looked away. *This can't be true.*

"Your son," the doctor began, and then paused to take a deep breath before continuing, "has a brain tumor. I'll give you some space." She put her hands on our shoulders as we huddled together, crying. Of all the things you never want to hear as a parent, that phrase is in the top three. *Your son has a brain tumor.* I couldn't comprehend it.

Savanna was going into shock. She rocked Hayes back and forth with her hands covering her face. I was pacing back and forth around the hospital room, trying to grasp the information we had just been given. I had no way of controlling my emotions in that moment, but I knew Savanna needed me. Hayes needed me. I stopped my pacing, bent down, and hugged Savanna as tight as I could with Hayes in between us. She was motionless, unable to find strength to squeeze me back. Our world had just stopped. It ended. We were both frozen in time.

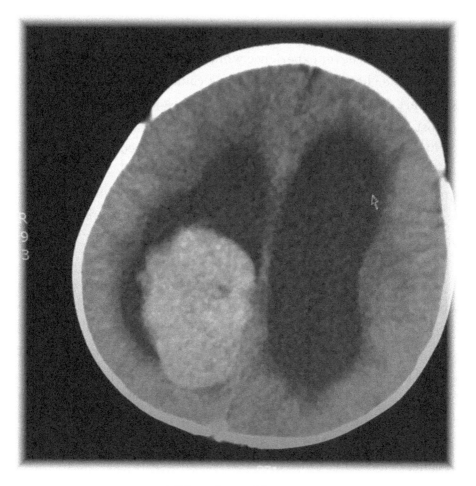

A CT-scan image of the tumor.

Some doctors opened the door slowly. "We are the Neuro team," one said as they entered. They were considerate of our space and the moment Savanna and I were sharing.

"We are going to perform surgery first thing in the morning," they said as they crouched down to make eye contact with us. "We will intubate him tonight, and get a full brain and spine MRI this evening while he is still under anesthesia." One of the physicians placed his hand on Savanna's shoulder. We failed to ask any questions. Our minds still hadn't thawed from the shock of seeing an image of the tumor. "We will take a biopsy during surgery and send it to pathology," he continued to talk as we tried to focus on what he was telling us.

"Is it cancerous?" I finally managed to ask shakily. I really didn't want to know the answer.

"We can't know until we go in for surgery. Like I mentioned, we will need to send tissue to pathology to determine whether it's benign or malignant," he replied. Our eyes were beginning to dry, and we wiped the remaining drops from our cheeks.

There's no dress rehearsal for a moment like this. We were both trying to comprehend the situation. After the Neuro team left, any conversation that occurred in that room was completely muffled, like something out of *The Peanuts Movie*. All we could do was sit there and stare at the white floor. We didn't want to accept the news— it was everything we had feared and more. I never envisioned a nightmare like this happening to our perfect family.

But in that hospital room, we received validation. We could finally understand the reason behind the instincts that had been pushing themselves at us for the past month. The impressions from God were letting us know it wasn't just a virus, it was a monster taking up a third of our little boy's brain.

With the MRI scheduled a few hours later, we needed to make arrangements for the other five kids. While we felt as though our minds and the world had been put on hold, our kids needed to be cared for. They needed some love and attention while we prepared to stay overnight with Hayes. So we picked up our phones and began having much-dreaded conversations with our close friends and loved ones—the first among many difficult updates about Hayes. My mind could barely function, so rehashing the turn of events for my relatives made things more difficult.

Tears flowed as I tried to explain things to my mom. "They found a tumor," I said. She cried in silence as I explained the details of the past hour. My mom tends to be completely silent when she is saddened or depressed, and her lack of words only made my mind wander to darker places. After an hour or so, we had made all the calls to secure love and support for our kids so we could center our focus on our baby boy.

Hayes was soon intubated and they took him back for the MRI. I felt the need to see my kids. I missed them. It had only been a few hours, but I craved holding them. I also wanted to be the one to tell them about Hayes. They had shared our concerns about him the entire time, and they deserved to be told by their Dad. So I rushed home while Savanna stayed with Hayes.

I drove toward home and turned up our street only to see a swarm of cars lining our fence, continuing up our driveway. I immediately felt love and support oozing from our home.

Another person who has been placed in our lives for something much greater than just a friendship or acquaintance is Krista Parry. She moved into the neighborhood with her family only months before the triplets were born. I pulled into my driveway as Krista was walking up to our front door. She stopped, looked back, saw me, and ran over to give me a hug.

"I'm so sorry Steve," she said as tears rolled down her cheeks. We walked inside together. The house was filled with kids and adults. It was our family, our giant Mormon family. Well, it was mostly Savanna's giant, Mormon family. The atmosphere was pure chaos, which I typically dread, but not at this moment. Instead, the noise balanced an afternoon full of complete, lonely silence. I welcomed it.

I searched for the kids and directed them to our upstairs bedroom. The older three were aware of what was happening, but I wanted to discuss it with them and answer any questions. I sat down next to them on my bed.

"As you know, we have been trying to find out why Hayes has been so sick," I said as I looked each of them in the eye. "We found out why he has been throwing up and acting so tired," I said, taking a deep breath before continuing. "Hayes has a tumor." I made sure to keep my cool and confidence with them. I take my job as a dad very seriously, and this was about to become one of the most important—yet difficult—conversations I would have with my children. It was to be the first of many.

Bo and Mia cried, and Wes sat there confused about what was going on. He was barely four years old, so I understood that he was more worried about his Nerf gun and the pizza that had been ordered for the kids.

"We have a great team of people who are going to help Hayes get better," I explained. I hugged them close to me and explained the plan for the night and the following morning, when they would be doing surgery on Hayes's brain. The kids were scared, but I could tell they felt much more at peace with Dad home. We all needed the physical and emotional interactions of this moment. We knelt down beside each other, said a prayer for baby Hayes, and left the room. I quickly thanked everyone for jumping in to help with the kids, and got back in the car to return to Savanna and Hayes.

Hayes was still sedated, as they had decided to keep him sedated throughout the night in preparation for surgery the next morning. I sat down next to Savanna. "I love you," I said, trying to somehow ease the pain. There aren't any words that you can say to alleviate what we were experiencing. She knew I loved her, but I needed to say it anyway. She stood up, hugged me, and told me that she loved me too. We were hot messes: my face was swollen and my eyes were as bloodshot as peppermint candy. Savanna's hair was all over the place and her mascara was smeared around her eyes. We were completely terrified.

Hayes was intubated in a hospital crib, and we shared a seat on the cheap hospital chair that also served as a foldout bed. We sat in silence, with only the beeping noise of the heartrate monitor in the background. I stared up at the ceiling, as if looking directly to God in search for some type of answer. I said a small prayer in my heart to get us out of this. We needed a miracle the following morning: one that would remove that beastly tissue consuming Hayes's brain.

Text messages flooded our phones. News was getting around and people were offering their condolences. My life has never been very private, due to my football career. I also did contract work at the local radio and television stations as a football analyst. So much of my life was made into public knowledge through my social media accounts. Savanna also used social media as a source of support for the triplets. Her triplet community offered support when things got crazy. That community had each other's back; you'd think they were part of the Italian mob from the way they showed up for one another.

But with hundreds of alerts going off, we put the phones on silent and ignored the messages. We were overwhelmed, and the thought of explaining the previous six hours to everyone seemed extremely daunting, but we also knew we needed support from those around us. We needed any help people were willing to offer. So rather than reply to every message we received, we sent out a brief summary of Hayes's condition on Instagram with the hashtags #hayestough #prayforHayes. It proved to be an excellent way to inform people without having to explain the entire story fifty-thousand times. I'm obviously exaggerating, I'm not that popular. It's probably more like forty-thousand times.

"How are we going to do this?" Savanna asked as she grabbed my hand firmly. She needed me to be strong, but my mind had been wandering off to some extremely dark places. I didn't know how to answer that question, but I tried my best to be the supportive, strong husband she needed as I looked her in the eyes.

"Babe, we are going to get through this," I said, confidently answering her question. But I was asking myself, *We're going to get through this? What does that even mean?* My mind began wondering again. I was trying to teach myself to control every thought, and the only way I could make my mind stay focused was by repeating a prayer to myself. It wasn't your typical, formal prayer like the ones I had been taught to say. It was a conversation with God, similar to one I would have with a friend: "God, if you're really there, please get us through this." I repeated that over and over in my head.

Savanna's phone said that Rick was calling from Idaho Falls. She ignored it since we weren't in the mood to talk to anyone. He called again. She sent it to voicemail and, rolling her eyes, tucked the phone in her pocket. When he called a third time, she felt as though she should talk to him. So she put the phone to her ear.

I couldn't hear the conversation, but I understood her body language and facial expressions. Her jaw dropped open as she placed her left hand over her mouth. She was in disbelief. The color in her cheeks began to fade—something serious was going on. She said goodbye as a new wave of tears began streaming down her cheeks.

She dropped the phone and fell into my arms. I was too scared to ask what she'd been told. I wasn't sure I could take any more punches to the face.

"It's on his spine too," she sobbed into my arm.

"What's on his spine?" I asked.

"The tumor. It's on his, it's...on...it's on his spine too," she said as her body shook. She had hardly been able to finish her sentence.

8

SURGERY

---

*H*ayes was sedated, resting peacefully, but seeing him with the tube in his mouth was alarming. There wasn't a lot of room in the ICU, but we weren't about to leave his side. So Savanna and I cuddled up next to each other, shifting back and forth periodically to avoid getting numb bums. We tried to keep each other calm with small talk, but no topic would ever take our minds off the events that were unfolding.

I stared at the clock as it ticked through the night. It was extremely uncomfortable in that hospital room, and the privacy was nonexistent. Across the hall was a teenage patient, with her mom and dad, who was obviously unstable. From overheard conversations between her doctor and parents, we knew she was suffering from some sort of mental illness. There was no way we were sleeping that night, especially because our neighbors made no attempt to quiet their voices as they talked about their child. We heard the word "suicide" several times. I felt terrible for the parents and for the girl who was battling those demons in her head.

We were experiencing an entirely new world that had seemed nonexistent just ten hours earlier. And I felt guilty. *Why?* I asked myself over and over as a sense of guilt filled my mind. Every person, every family has their own issues, and I felt as though I had been unaware of people's needs prior to that night. The overwhelming need to be a better father, husband, neighbor, coworker, and friend obsessed me. This experience was changing me. Reality was hitting hard. So I felt guilty for taking the previous nine months of Hayes's life for granted. I knew, that first night, that our lives were never going to be the same. It's amazing how fast things can change. I made a promise to myself: from that moment forward, I would never take a day for granted. I promised to embrace each day and to appreciate normality. I still hold myself accountable to that promise.

We had no idea what the new norm was going to be. Those were the thoughts I tried to control, but my mind was extremely undisciplined. I was trying to channel my "inner Savanna" to imbue some positivity, and my mind simply wandered off like an untrained puppy. I considered what life would be like if Hayes didn't make it. I tried everything in my power to avoid those thoughts; when they crept in, I even physically shook my head to clear them.

At one point, I took a walk. Hayes was peacefully sleeping and I needed to get out of that room. I found myself all alone on the second floor of the hospital. There's nothing as lonely as a hospital in the middle of the night. A shiver filled my body as I paced up and down the hall. I was trying to occupy my mind by focusing on something happy. *My kids make me happy,* I thought, and I began daydreaming our typical daily routine when we play with babies and pass them back and forth. I daydreamed about a healthy Hayes, filled with smiles and laughter, but that kept getting interrupted by mental flashes of the CT-scan image. It would jump in uninvited, without warning. The picture was etched in my brain, because that ugly tumor was standing in the way of my son and his future.

I despised every minute of that lonely night. I found an unattended hallway, sat down next to a blue neon sign, and began to sob uncontrollably. I had never felt more alone than that moment, when I sat on the hospital floor with my back against the wall. *What did I do to deserve this?* I stared down at the floor with tears falling from my eyes. Then I felt a presence close to me, and peered up to see Savanna. She knelt, put her head on my shoulder, and kissed my cheek.

"I love you," she said as she cuddled in closer.

We made our way back to the room around 4:30 a.m. Savanna dozed off for an hour as I browsed my phone. It was the only way I could occupy my mind. I pulled up Instagram and saw a red 100+ notification on the bottom right of the screen. I had never received that many notifications about a post before. I read each and every message that had come in throughout the night. It amazed me. We were receiving so much love. Some of the messages came from complete strangers. I knew we were loved, and it felt calming. The positivity filled my soul. It was as if my tank was on empty and these little messages were fueling my heart into a healthier state. It was completely therapeutic. I have always had a love-hate relationship with social media, but that night I saw the goodness of that world. I felt an incredible amount of love and support. And as strange as it sounds, for the first time, I felt hope.

In those moments, there was a distinct two-way connection I felt between me and the people following along on Instagram. At first, I was hesitant to share this extremely raw and emotional event, but there was an undeniable need to do it. Yes, I wanted to benefit from the support. I also wanted to allow others to gain perspective on life without having to actually live through such a crisis. I felt compelled to share what had happened earlier that afternoon, to share our perspective on everything, to share my emotions. So I did. Maybe it was therapy for me, who knows. But whatever the reason was, I was following the same intuitive prompting that pushed me to get Hayes help in the first place.

Around 6 a.m., Savanna and I made our way down to the cafeteria. Savanna hadn't eaten in 24 hours and I had only managed a few forkfuls of rice during lunch with Mike Greene. We had absolutely zero appetite but we needed to put something in our stomach to give us some sort of energy. I needed something in my system to avoid going crazy, which tends to happen when I don't eat. We've all seen those Snickers commercials where the main character appears to have split personalities before eating the candy bar. Yeah, that is me. I needed some food in my system before I went Jekyll and Hyde on Savanna or the hospital staff. We tried to find something, anything that looked appealing. We both felt guilty for eating that morning. It was as if we were making an extremely selfish decision to feed our faces while our son was about to go in for a life-altering surgery. Our entire focus was on Hayes, so the thought of doing something for ourselves was extremely unappealing. It was the first time in my life that I've ever felt guilty for eating. We split a 200-calorie granola bar and walked back upstairs to ICU room 28.

While the OR was being prepped, a surgeon came in to talk to us. "I believe there is a solid lining that separates the tumor from the other tissue of the brain." His tone was confident. "If that's the case, we can remove the tumor entirely. We will do everything we can to remove the entire tumor. I will spend as much time as I physically can, as long as Hayes's body can handle it." He went on to inform us of the risks associated with this surgery, including death and the need for multiple blood transfusions. Of course we agreed to whatever risks there were. What was the alternative? Our hope was entirely in the hands of this team. We were handing over our son, our little underdog.

The doctors were ready for Hayes just after 9 a.m. He was still calmly sedated as we kissed him on the forehead. Then they wheeled him down the hallway. We interlocked hands and watched them go the entire distance with tears rolling down our faces. The team of surgeons seemed extremely confident. They had an arrogance to them, and why wouldn't they? They were brain surgeons. We knew they were going to take care of Hayes and do their best to remove the tumor.

We went to the Ronald McDonald house to wait during the surgery. It was a fairly new room in the hospital, built for people like us who were spending long days and nights there and needed some comfort. The room had a calming atmosphere. There was carpet, a fireplace, and some couches that overlooked downtown Salt Lake City. We could tell a lot of time and thought was put into that room to give family members an escape from reality. Maybe it was just an escape from those pathetic hospital chairs. We made that our base for the hours to come. A few members of Savanna's family joined us while we waited. They kept us company with some small talk, and I was appreciative to have them by my side as emotional support. I welcomed it after the longest night I had experienced in my life.

Savanna was having an extremely hard time waiting. Her hands never left her face. I wrapped my arms around her several times in an attempt to engage in conversation, but she was in a different world. I wanted to take her pain away, but there was nothing I could do at that moment. All we could do was wait and hope that things were going smoothly.

We saw waves of people come and go. I was jealous of them, jealous of the smiles on their faces. *How lucky they are!* I thought as they smiled and conversed with one another. I wondered if I would ever smile again. I wondered if I was ever going to be happy again. I felt guilty eating a freaking granola bar that tasted like cardboard. Horrible.

I was pondering whether I would ever experience real happiness again when Savanna's phone vibrated in her pocket.

"Steve!" she said, showing me the screen on her phone. "It's the hospital."

My heart was racing as I stood up to do my usual bull-in-the-ring pacing. It didn't seem right for them to be calling yet. I looked down at my watch and did the math. We had been told this surgery could take as long as eight hours, but we had only been waiting for two hours and twelve minutes.

"Okay, we'll be right there," she said. There was no additional information. The person who called was just the middleman, informing us that the surgery was over. Extreme doubt and excitement both flooded me as we picked up our things and made our way to the recovery room.

"Well, that's gotta be a good sign," my father-in-law said.

"Yeah, you're probably right," Savanna said in response, trying to believe it. But the word *probably* was key—it meant there was hesitation, a reason for doubt. We were doubting everything at this point. We had just been through the most emotional night of our lives so there was nothing we didn't question.

I felt excited about the quickness of the surgery. "It has to be a good sign, right?" I asked Savanna, hoping for validation or reassurance. Savanna is the optimistic one in the relationship, but unfortunately she was experiencing the same set of emotions as me. So my thoughts drifted to other possibilities. Maybe it meant they couldn't go any further because of his tiny body. Maybe it was too much to continue moving forward. An emotional tug-of-war was going on in my head as we walked down the hall to the recovery area. We waited for the surgeon to arrive and deliver the news.

I watched the surgeon walk toward us, observing his every move. This guy was good, he didn't give off any hint of what had happened in that operating room.

"Let's find a quiet room," he said, and we fell into step behind him. *What does that mean?* I thought. Does that mean he needed to deliver some bad news? If it was good news then why wasn't he high-fiving us in the hallway? He found an unoccupied room and we sat down, hearts racing. I could see Savanna's pulse in her neck and it was congruent with mine. I guessed we were about three heartbeats away from going into cardiac arrest.

"We were able to remove the tumor," he said with a stoic look on his face. "We can never be 100 percent positive until we do additional images, but I'm extremely confident we were able to get its entirety." Joy, pure joy, rushed my system. I grabbed Savanna and she fell into my arms in complete relief and happiness. We were so happy. We held that embrace for a few seconds before allowing him to finish.

"We will send the tissue to pathology but, judging by the makeup of this tumor, I'd say it's malignant." The emotional roller-coaster car suddenly ran us over. The joy escaped our bodies and we were immediately filled with sorrow once again. He informed us that Hayes was doing well and resting in the recovery unit. We thanked him with handshakes of appreciation, sincere in our gratitude. I felt genuine love for him; he helped our baby boy.

As the surgeon left the room, we sat in silence for a moment trying to digest the news. We had just found out our baby likely had cancer. That had been the biggest rush of joy, then sorrow, alternating in seconds. This was the first of many emotional roller coasters that we would experience throughout our entire journey. Daily life was to be filled with an array of emotions. There were so many moments of fear and doubt, followed by moments of excitement and happiness. Joy and pride followed by anger and sorrow. This was the beginning of an emotional war.

We had a decision to make as a married couple and, more importantly, a mom and dad. We now knew a battle with cancer and its treatments was ahead. What emotion was going to drive us? Were we going to allow doubt and fear to control our lives for the remainder of this recovery? That sounded miserable. I couldn't fathom waking up each morning with that burden on my brain, controlling my every move. Or were we going to cling to every ounce of happiness and hope, and let that fuel us? Waking up to brightness, love and hope sounded much livelier. It would create memories as a family.

I had this vivid debate in my head as we sat in silence in the empty room. This was a decision I needed to make, but not for myself. It was for Hayes and the other five children who looked to me for support and leadership. I chose the latter option. I was going to cling to the positives and fight like hell to escape any negatives that tried to enter my brain.

Hayes was still under anesthesia, recovering, so we ran downstairs to get some actual food. We were thrilled that the evil monster of a tumor was gone from his body. It was almost as though the cancer part of our conversation with the surgeon didn't happen. Maybe it was denial, or maybe we were focused on winning an extremely important advance in this battle.

We allowed ourselves to breathe for the first time in 24 hours. A weight had lifted from our shoulders and our hope was restored. We even felt good enough to have a Coke Zero, a tender mercy that the hospital provided. Our appetites were restored and the guilt was erased. It's amazing how much emotion can prevent or allow us to do things. This lesson would soon become very clear, as when driven by negative emotions, we were unable to eat, drink, or even shower at times. They left us empty inside. They physically wore us down. On the other hand, when we felt hope and happiness, we could actually live. It may not have been our previous definition of living, but the positive view allowed us to wake up each morning and function each day.

We headed back upstairs after only a few minutes in the cafeteria. We walked in the room as Hayes was beginning to awaken. It felt so good to see him, it was as if I was meeting him for the first time. Flashbacks of his birth filled my mind. He still had the breathing tube in his mouth, but his closed eyelids began to move as he tried to open them.

"Hi, my baby boy," Savanna said as she placed her hand on his forehead. He immediately opened his eyes. His eyes were swollen, and they filled with tears. They weren't tears of sorrow, they were from the joy of seeing us. I walked to the other side of his crib and was overcome with a feeling that seemed to be coming directly from Hayes. It was gratitude. He was letting us know how grateful he was that we had listened to our parental instincts. I felt him thanking us for not listening when we were told it was just a virus. In that moment, I connected with Hayes in a way I had never connected to any of my children. It was as if our souls were one and the same. The feeling I received from him was undeniable; I have no doubt that Hayes spoke directly to me. Hayes was a special boy, almost "out of this world" special, and this moment confirmed that.

Around 2 a.m. that night, we couldn't sleep so we made our way back to Hayes's room. The nurse was doing a routine follow-up with some white noise in the background. We looked down at Hayes and saw a blank stare in his eyes. They were open and focused. It was an eerie type of focus, a wide-open gaze, not looking at any particular object. His mouth was slightly open and his tongue was moving back and forth against his two front teeth. He appeared extremely abnormal. Savanna and I looked at each other and peered back again at Hayes. We shared the same uneasy feeling.

The nurse was busy administering some medication. She could sense our concern and came over to examine Hayes. "Does he usually play with his tongue like that at home?" she asked, trying to assess the situation.

"No, we've never seen him do that," Savanna replied quickly. "Is he having a seizure?" she asked with a confident, yet startled, inflection in her voice. The nurse immediately paged the Neuro team, and they rushed over. We were witnessing Hayes have a seizure. We observed him intensely for a few minutes and tried to snap him out of it, or calm him down. We talked to him quietly and rubbed his cheeks. Whatever we were doing seemed to work. The haze from his eyes faded and he began to relax to tone of our voices. Just as the medical team arrived, Hayes fell back asleep. His eyes were closed and his body was relaxed. They asked us a few questions about the event and planned a follow-up the next morning. Apparently seizures were extremely common after brain surgery, especially with the size of tumor that Hayes had.

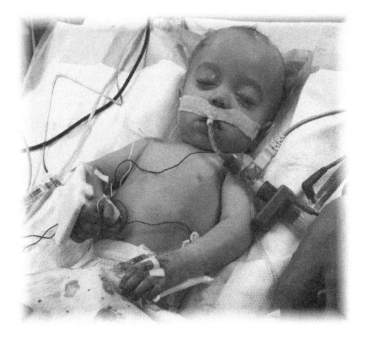

Hayes, moments after his tumor was removed.

In the days following his surgery, Hayes made progress. We could see glimpses of the old Hayes coming back, which filled my heart with extreme happiness. Hayes had a small, stuffed frog in his room. I would grab the frog and make regular attempts to get him to laugh. It's a dad's job to make his kids laugh, so I worked hard at it.

I was playing peekaboo with Hayes as I moved the frog up for him to see, and then down to vanish behind the crib. He began to giggle softly. I kept going and eventually he burst into classic Hayes laughter. He was laughing! It filled the hospital room, and it filled my entire heart. It had been almost eight weeks since I had heard Hayes's laugh and it immediately recharged me. It was as if someone had taken the defibrillator from the hospital wall and zapped me with it. Hayes was laughing! I threw the stuffed frog in the air and kissed him on the forehead. I wanted to kiss everyone at that moment. Our little Hayes was laughing and finally beginning to feel like his old self again.

9

ONE IN THREE MILLION

*A*bout a week after Hayes's surgery, they started prepping him to go home. The kids were thrilled at the idea of having their brother back. They hadn't been able to visit him since it was in the heart of flu season and visitors under the age of fourteen were prohibited. Hayes was doing really well recovering in the Neuro Trauma Unit. He was able to sit up with just a little assistance, and the physical and occupational therapy teams came in a few times to get him out of bed and engaged in activities. I was surprised by their urgency to get him out of bed, given he just had major brain surgery.

I was extremely cautious with Hayes after surgery. I had never been like that with any of my kids before. I'm a big believer in allowing children to learn failure because sometimes they needed to experience a little heartache and pain. Maybe I'm old school, but that's how I was raised. I grew into a contributing citizen, so my parent's way of nurturing seems to work just fine. If it's not broken, don't fix it. But I was overly protective with Hayes because of everything we had been through with him. I knew he was a fighter, so the immediate need to do physical therapy seemed premature.

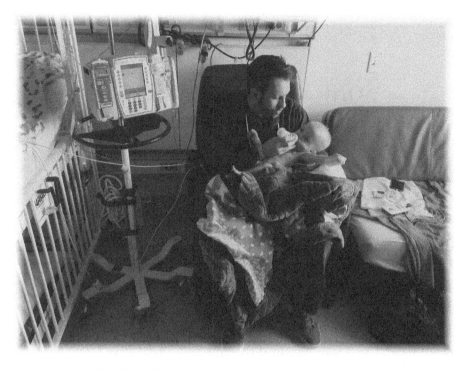

Me holding Hayes following one of his many physical therapy sessions.

I observed Hayes as they worked with him. He knew nothing better than to follow their leads. His innocence was actually helping him get stronger, whereas some adults—including me—would decline the therapy only four days after major brain surgery. But not Hayes, he did it. I was witnessing his resiliency. He was tough, #Hayestough. It actually taught me a valuable lesson about not feeling sorry for yourself in the midst of the circumstance you're facing. I was learning some incredibly valuable lessons from my ten-month-old boy. Typically the dad teaches the son how to handle difficult situations, but it wasn't that way with Hayes. His innocence was refreshing; he felt extraordinary. Hayes didn't feel sorry for himself. He never balked when they lifted him from his crib to do the physical therapy. There was no voice that said, "This is too hard" or "This isn't fair." He didn't know any alternative. As adults, we know the alternative, and it's called "taking the path of least resistance." We tend to avoid hard things. Unlike Hayes, we have that voice in our heads, and we tend to let it win by giving in when life feels too hard. Adults have excuses. But there were absolutely no excuses from Hayes.

When the doctors finally said we could bring Hayes home, I dashed home to go tell the kids. All six of us jumped in the Suburban to pick him up, babies included. We were in this fight together and I wanted to make sure Hayes knew he had the entire family behind him. The kids had made signs that read, "Get well soon Hayes," another read "Hayestough," and Wes carried one with a giant heart that had Hayes inside it. It was a classic, childlike picture with a circle head and four sticks poking out for arms and legs. It lacked some detail, as you would expect from a boy who recently turned four, but Wes had drawn the battle scar that Hayes had earned on his head—one that would tell a story the rest of his life. Bo was also excited to see Hayes's scar. It is every boy's dream to have something like that to flash around. Scars seem to represent an initiation into manhood.

At the hospital, the kids sat on a bench in the main entrance and peered down the hall to get first glimpse of Hayes. "There he is!" Bo shouted as he ran to see him. Bo is an incredible older brother. While he is one of the best football players I have ever seen at his age, he has a sensitive side to him when he's home with his siblings. He was extremely compassionate, worrying about Hayes as if he was a parent.

Mia and Wes followed Bo to see Hayes, who was grinning from ear to ear with joy. It was clear he was relieved to see his older siblings. We took some heartwarming pictures, posted them on Instagram, and headed home. The drive was filled with absolute excitement. Our family was back together again! It felt like we had been given a second chance at life.

As I was driving, I peered up at an overpass bridge that provided a means for children to avoid crossing heavy traffic on their way to Churchill Junior High school. It was the same school where Savanna and I had first met. Hanging from the bridge was a sign that read "Hayestough." I couldn't believe my eyes.

I yelled back to the kids to point it out. I immediately knew who did it: our neighbor, Krista. She's a real go-getter, with a personality that could light up a cave. She's one of the most genuine people I've ever met, and she made us feel special that day. Hayes had no idea there were signs lining the street and green bows on telephone poles, but I'm sure he felt the love and support the rest of us were taking in. We had always felt that green was Hayes's color. He couldn't talk, but if he could I'm sure he would've told us that his favorite color was green.

Krista had also arranged for the entire neighborhood to greet us as we made our way to our street. All these genuinely kind, considerate people lined the street to greet us on that cold January evening. Tears rolled down my face as I watched each of them cheering us on as we drove up. It was a special moment for our entire family. Savanna rolled down her window to say thank you to all the people. That lonely week in the hospital had worn us out, and we craved this social interaction.

Hayes with his triplet brother and sister after returning home from surgery.

We knew we were just beginning this war against the disease in Hayes's body, but we were determined to celebrate each milestone. This was our first, giant milestone. We hadn't even received the pathology report back, but in some weird way it didn't consume our thoughts. We were partying and nothing else mattered. Focused on the good things and living in the now—that had been the theme since Hayes's tumor was removed. So we agreed to keep a good thing going.

Seeing Hayes home with his siblings was incredible. They were observing him from head to toe. He was a hot commodity, everyone wanted his attention. The boys checked out his scar and asked questions about the surgery. We did our best to answer their questions, but they hardly seemed interested in what we had to say. They were just thrilled to have their little brother back. With everyone together, it was a perfect opportunity to discuss the road ahead. We didn't know what type of treatment was to come, but we did know it was going to be long and extensive. I wanted to prepare the kids for future days and possibly nights without their mom or dad.

"As you know, they were able to remove Hayes tumor, and we are really excited about that," I said focusing on my tone and doing my best to stay positive. "How amazing is it to have Hayes back home?" I asked. It was a rhetorical question to build up the positivity and confidence. They all agreed, it was exciting. "So, even though Hayes's tumor is gone," I paused for a second, trying to gather up enough courage to say that awful C-word. I continued, "Hayes has cancer." I held back the tears and stayed strong, but I was pained to my bones.

That was the first time I had said those words out loud. I knew the kids were waiting for some kind of follow up. I was looking directly in their eyes, as the leader of the house. That gave me the courage to keep going. "We are going to get Hayes better." I said confidently, drawing on my previous experience of motivating football teams. "We are going to get Hayes the help he needs to beat cancer." I said, chest outstretched and chin up. "And after we get him all better," I continued, "we will go to Disneyland to celebrate." Game over, drop the freaking mic! It was the best speech I had given in my entire life. The kids were extremely animated and confident going into our uphill climb, and we were ready to take this beast on.

Ten days passed. Ten days of blissful normality. We were picking up the pieces and life seemed to be calm, though we were dreading the call about the pathology report. I was at the office when Savanna called with the doctor on the line.

"It's what we expected," he said. "He has choroid plexus carcinoma, a cancer that lives in the membranes. I expect the oncology team will be reaching out soon to start chemotherapy."

"When do we start chemotherapy?" we asked simultaneously.

"I'm not sure what the exact protocol is, but I will make sure that someone contacts you to answer additional questions and give you dates for treatment."

We thanked him and said our goodbyes. The conversation had been very vague, and I stared at my notes that included the name of the diagnosis. "Choroid plexus carcinoma" stared back at me while my mind raced with curiosity. I picked up my iPhone and for the first time and the absolute last time, I typed the diagnosis into the search engine.

What popped up on my screen almost caused me to pass out. I remember every detail of our journey with this cancer, but I cannot for the life of me remember the details from that google search. It was the negativity I was training myself to ignore, so I've erased it from my memory bank. All I know is that the information was extremely discouraging and depressing. I had spent the past ten days in a blissful paradise filled with hope and strength, and one small internet search caused it all to come crashing down. It destroyed my hope.

In the past weeks, I had learned that hope is the one thing to cling to, the emotion to hold onto. It had become the quarterback directing the offense in my brain. All I had was hope, so when the google search destroyed it, life felt dark and helpless. I knew I couldn't live in that gray, lonely world of despair; I had made a promise to focus on the positive and steer the negatives out of my mind. This was both the first time and the last time that negative thoughts won a battle in this war.

My heart sank to my stomach as I stood by my desk. My fingers tingled and my vision became blurry. The blood rushed from my head and I knew my face was about to get carpeted so I scurried to sit down. Fortunately I was able to catch myself with my right arm on the desk and use my other hand to guide my rear end onto the leather chair. One thought remained in my mind: Hayes's cancer happened in one child for every three million children. It was rare!

10

TREATMENT OPTIONS

I came home from the office that day completely depleted. Savanna was on the computer researching everything she could about this type of cancer. She was much stronger than I was when it came to statistics. She didn't let the bad prognosis statistics affect her, while I work in an industry that is very statistically driven. In the financial world, we use statistics to helps us assess the risk and reward of investing. Statistics are extremely meaningful to me. I had also spent the past three weeks training my every thought to remain positive, so reading anything discouraging was a threat to my mental health.

Savanna did the researching on her own, learning about treatment protocols and success rates. In a few days, she had already learned the nuances of the chosen protocol that the team of oncologists soon proposed to us. And we turned to a Facebook support group for guidance on the available options. People suggested various institutions and we had already heard exceptional things about St. Jude Children's Research Hospital in Memphis, Tennessee. They were doing a study on various types of brain cancers, including the one Hayes had. It sounded like perfect timing, so we got in touch with the research coordinator at St. Jude. We were exploring all our options prior to meeting with the team at Primary Children's Hospital, so we looked at the protocols at both hospitals. While we felt relief knowing all the options available, it was extremely difficult to decide between staying home or going to Memphis. Both protocols required six months of chemotherapy.

Chemotherapy was a chapter in the journey that I dreaded. I didn't want to watch my son lose his hair and experience near-lethal side effects. It was feeling like every time we got comfortable and confident about life, we had to face a new step in the process that brought hard emotions and feelings. The thought of cancer has always scared me as a parent. In fact, it scared me as a child. I always feared that the evil C-word would play some sort of role in my future. Savanna was diagnosed with thyroid cancer when she was fifteen years old. We were both sophomores, and the news was hard for me to understand. Savanna was the only young person I knew who had cancer. We spent a lot of our dating days talking about our future together, and I feared that she would get cancer or pass cancer down to our children. I was obviously naive and didn't understand exactly how cancer develops in young children. Regardless, I had an ongoing impression that it would affect me in some way.

I was having a hard time telling people my son had cancer. When I told the social media world that Hayes had cancer on January 20th, it was extremely difficult. I asked for their prayers and thoughts, and began asking God for a miracle.

On the morning of our appointment with the oncology team at Primary Children's, I was nervous and so was Savanna. We loaded Hayes in the car and started our drive to the hospital. I peered out my window as the cars passed me. I was driving slow, soaking up all the freedom in that moment before chemotherapy began. One car passed us on the left and I noticed the passenger. She was beautiful, probably in her mid-twenties, and she was bald. She too was battling cancer.

That image was vivid. It immediately made me ponder how prevalent this disease is. When I parked the car, I tapped a description into my notes app and added: "Life is too sensitive to take for granted."

We made our way to the fourth floor of the hospital where the bone marrow and cancer unit was located. I saw the signs for the cancer unit and immediately felt depressed. It was another reality check. As we entered the clinic for the first time on January 26th, I gazed around the waiting room at all the amazing, cancer-fighting children with bald heads. We were now a part of this world, one that had previously seemed nonexistent.

I saw the fight in the kids' eyes, and I also saw innocence. Each gaze seemed to tell a story, one much bigger than the frame of a young body. These kids didn't deserve cancer. Nobody deserves cancer, but especially not them. Cancer is evil. I suddenly felt angry that all these kids had to go through aggressive treatments that kill every fast-growing cell in their bodies. Their youth was being stolen by this monstrous disease. I also felt extreme empathy as I began thinking about our little boy, who would soon lose his hair. It scared me to know that he would be part of this club. Not because of his appearance, I couldn't care less about that. I was scared because a bald head meant that he actually had cancer. The reality of this world was starting to sink in.

That day was overwhelmed with information about the next steps for Hayes, and for the next chapter in our lives. The oncologist was well-prepared for our meeting and extremely considerate of our desire to explore the options available at St. Jude Children's Hospital. She even compared the different protocols. At St. Jude, Hayes would receive six months of extreme chemotherapy followed by six months of chemotherapy administered at home. Locally, the protocol was six months of intense chemotherapy followed by a stem-cell transplant. It was called the Head Start II protocol, and had a good track record of sending kids into remission. Since the surgery, Savanna had been reaching out to parents who chose this protocol and they all recommended it.

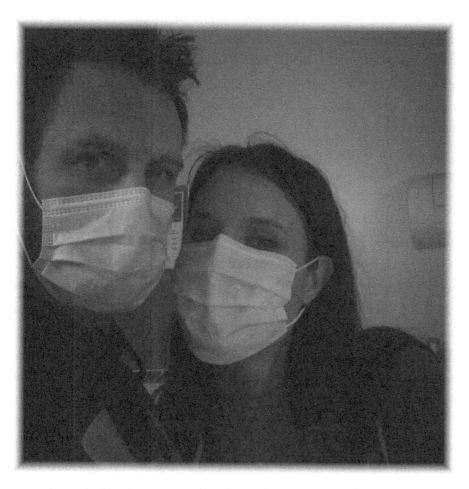

Savanna and me during the first round of chemotherapy.

One mother advised, "Choose the most aggressive protocol presented to you. I have found too many children relapse due to a lack of aggressiveness in the beginning." It was excellent advice that helped us during our decision-making process.

The oncologist had a calm confidence that we appreciated. She had even treated this type of cancer two times before. That doesn't sound like a lot, but we were thrilled that she had any experience treating this extremely rare type of cancer. We asked her how those two children were doing now.

"Both are doing well," she replied confidently, and we felt reassured.

Prior to the meeting, Savanna and I had been leaning toward St. Jude. In fact, we were expecting to catch a flight a few days later to begin the therapy for Hayes. We had already spoken with the kids about it, telling them that mom and Hayes were going to live in Tennessee for the next six months. They had no objections, being as committed to helping their little brother as we were.

We headed home and discussed the options with each other, weighing pros and cons as we went to bed. With so much on our minds, we couldn't sleep so we kept talking. We were trying to feel each other out. I was hesitant to let her know exactly how I felt because I didn't want to persuade her.

We discussed the next six months. While we feared being apart for so long, we were willing to fly to China for a cure if we had to. The babies were in a prime developmental stage, learning to rollover and beginning to arch their little bums in the air, preparing to crawl. I knew Savanna would miss all of this if she was in Memphis, which was impossible to imagine. We definitely didn't want to uproot the entire family and rip the kids from the normality of activities and school. They were dealing with extremely hard stuff and needed their support systems. They needed friends and relatives close by.

We both had the sense that the protocol at Primary Children's Hospital was more aggressive. This was extremely appealing to us.

It sounds harsh, but we wanted to all-out attack this beast to avoid any possibility of relapse. I felt like we were on the same page about a decision, but neither of us wanted to admit it yet. We were worn out and eventually dozed off.

I woke up the next morning with clarity and immediately told Savanna that I felt it was best to undergo treatment locally. I believed we were being pushed to stay home with the support of friends and family. The protocol was proven and the most aggressive. Savanna said she felt the exact same way. While it was fairly rare for us to disagree, I felt instantaneous relief. Our instincts were telling us this was the best route, and we had learned not to deny them. We were staying home!

The kids were thrilled when we told them. I had been extremely proud of their willingness to sacrifice their Mom to help their little brother, and was glad to remove that worry from their minds. Our kids had maturity much greater than their ages. They were selfless and considerate of Hayes's needs. I felt our bond as a family grow during this difficult decision-making process. Each of us was committed to helping Hayes, and everyone was willing to sacrifice. Maybe it was the Disneyland promise, but whatever motivated them was working.

I am not opposed to bribing my children. Wes was monitoring Hayes's scar, and every morning he would wake up and inspect it. "Dad, he's getting better," he said that day. "I think we can go to Disneyland tomorrow!" I encouraged his optimism. I could've used a few doses of it as we headed into the first round of chemotherapy.

11

CHEMOTHERAPY

On January 31, we checked Hayes into Primary Children's Hospital to start chemo treatments. It was something we had been dreading, but it was also a relief to start the fight against cancer. We were charged with hope, and ready to take on this challenge. Each new phase was one step closer to healing him, and every step brought additional hope. We had loved having him home after the tumor was removed, but that was, in some way, wasting precious time. The doctors believed Hayes needed time to recover from the surgery, so the moments leading up to this day had been full of anxiety. Hayes would be in the hospital for three consecutive weeks, then come home to recover before starting a new round.

We had been extremely blessed with people around us who were ready to jump in and help our family get through this. With them, we made plans for the next six months. Savanna was going to stay at the hospital and I determined to keep working. Someone had to pay the bills, especially since they were mounting with the medical attention Hayes needed. Also, I worked alongside my dad and I still felt like I had to prove myself to him. My days started around 6:30 a.m., when I would get up and showered before the babies started yelling at me for food. I would feed everybody and send the older kids out the door for school. Every morning seemed like a marathon, a full day of events crammed in by 9 a.m., just in time to start my day at the office. My mom would come to the house to take care of the babies and stay with Wes until around noon. Then one of Hayes's many aunts would come to fill the three hours until Veronica showed up. Veronica was someone we had been introduced to months earlier, who had experience helping with triplets. She was another person whose path crossed ours for reasons. She was a Godsend.

That was our schedule for six months of our lives. Sounds exhausting? Well, it was. This is just a small glimpse of the army that helped our family. They were Hayes's Army.

After we checked into the hospital, we immediately made our way to prep for surgery. They had to put in the central line, an access port that would direct medicine into Hayes's heart, which would then pump it throughout his entire body. It was the last time we saw our baby's chest without tubing attached for seven months.

The surgery went as planned and they showed us to a room on the fourth floor. There was a dry-erase board that read, "Welcome Hayes." The nurses were enthusiastic and made us comfortable by bringing some water and handing us additional information about the various medicines he would be receiving. There were four pages full of different medicines and the side effects that can come along with them. I didn't bother flipping through any of the pages, as I have more of a big-picture mindset. Those details seemed to only get in the way of my main focus: getting Hayes healthy.

Hayes playing in his crib during chemo, Round 1.

Morning came and so did Hayes's first dose of chemotherapy, which turned out to be pretty anticlimactic. It was administered through his central line and came in a brown bag that they often hung from an IV pole. Depending on the type of medicine, it was administered over three to four hours. There were all kinds of chemo medicines that Hayes had to take.

My days dragged on at the office. I found myself texting Savanna constantly for play-by-play updates on how Hayes was doing. She would send me pictures, and it was amazing how much I looked forward to seeing him. Each picture she sent to me included his angelic smile, even during his sickest days. Hayes was finding joy in being with his mom and dad, and we were taking advantage of every single moment with him. I would leave the office around 4 p.m., rush home to say hi to the kids, change my clothes, and head to the hospital. The first few days of that drive were filled with tears as I tried to process this new life. The reality of it all seemed to hit me when I was alone in the car. I felt like that was the only safe place for me to let it all out. I'm sure I got a lot of weird looks as people passed me, but it was my safe haven. I would cry the entire drive to the hospital, but made sure to stop and wipe my eyes before I saw Savanna.

Every day, as I made my way to switch places with Savanna for the evening, I would pass the U of U football stadium. Rice Eccles Stadium was where I used to run out of the tunnel in football pads as 46,000 people cheered. Now it marked the spot where I needed to start drying my eyes so Savanna wouldn't see the pain I was in. I needed to be strong for her. This fight wasn't about me at all—I wanted her entire focus to be on Hayes, not worried about what I was going through. I felt that we could worry about our feelings later.

At the hospital, I would open the car door for Savanna, give her a hug and kiss, and watch her drive off as she headed home to be with the kids. I would then head upstairs to be with Hayes for the next five hours.

The first round seemed to be going smoothly. I observed Hayes's every action to determine if he was in pain or experiencing any side effects. He was extremely happy every day, and we spent each hour laughing and smiling at each other. From the way he acted, you would never guess what he was going through. After ten days some of the side effects began surfacing, including sores in his throat.

Chemotherapy is brutal, almost barbaric. As I watched the medicine being administered, it amazed me that this was the only way to save Hayes. That terrible poison was our only hope for a healthy life. We were basically killing off the very essence of his little body to help him survive that dreaded disease. Each morning and night, we coated his mouth with a prescribed mouthwash to alleviate the pain from the sores, but it didn't seem to help. I could see that he was in intense pain. His poor little body was extremely uncomfortable, tossing and turning, back and forth, trying to find some sort of relief.

One morning they noticed some abnormalities in his blood sample. Apparently it's pretty typical for a virus to appear, especially when white blood cell counts are low. The doctor prescribed an antibiotic to fight off any infection. Still in some serious pain, Hayes's face began turning crimson red and his little hands were itching intensely. I panicked in my inability to help him. Standing next to his crib, feeling helpless, I tried everything I could to make him feel better. Nothing seemed to get his mind off what his body was going through. The side effects were in full effect.

I'll sing him a song, I thought, which is a terrible idea generally. I'm completely tone deaf. In seventh grade I had to take a required chorus class, and the teacher urged me to mouth the words to avoid displeasing the audience. Despite this, I was willing to do whatever it took to help Hayes, so I started singing some nursery rhymes. I put my hand on his forehead to soothe him and immediately felt extreme heat radiating from his forehead and saw beads of sweat forming around his little nose. Hayes must be having an allergic reaction to the antibiotic. I was really panicking now. I looked upward and begged God to make it stop so I could know what to do. I swung open the door and demanded a physician's attention. Hayes was in an abnormal amount of pain. My patience was out; I had been pushed to my edge. I had no worries about hurting anyone's feeling through the tone of my voice. I was Hayes's advocate and needed to be his voice. I was his only hope for communicating the discomfort he was in.

Despite moments like this, I continued to be impressed by how resilient Hayes was. Due to the severity and intensity of this type of cancer, Hayes was receiving the heaviest, most aggressive chemotherapy that could be given to a human being. And he was being a trooper.

During the first round of treatments, I formed a great relationship with a physician assistant named was Micah, who was a former collegiate soccer player. She would come into the room just to talk and check on Hayes, even if she wasn't assigned to care for him that day. Her heart was in her career. When Hayes was having a hard day, she often served as a therapist for us. There was a level of trust with Micah that I didn't have with most of the oncologists. Her eyes were compassionate, and she spoke to us on a parental level rather than using the more typical medical terminology.

One day, she explained to us just how intense the chemotherapy rounds were going to be for Hayes. She wasn't trying to scare us—she was appreciating Hayes's resiliency. "An adult wouldn't survive the amount of chemo that Hayes needs," she said to us on one of her off-duty visits. We had known his treatments were intense, but her comment immediately put things into perspective. The intensity and toxicity of his chemo medicine was why our hospital stays during each round were so long. Each type of cancer is different, and the treatment approach differs from patient to patient. For example, a child with leukemia never typically spent more than a few days at the hospital during their rounds. But Hayes was becoming a near-permanent hospital resident.

I hate to bore you with the details of each particular round, but I find it necessary to explain how they worked. For the first eight days, Hayes was given a total of six different chemotherapy drugs, each with their own side effects. One of the drugs made a catheter necessary so Hayes's urine wouldn't burn his skin worse than any third-degree burn. After day eight, there was no more chemotherapy. We would spend the remaining days waiting for his white blood cell count to drop completely, and then rebound to a level safe enough for Hayes to go home. While his white blood cell counts were down, he was extremely susceptive to infections, both bacterial and viral. They would draw his blood every other day to analyze how his body was reacting.

This was the routine for six months of our lives. After Round 1, we knew when and how his body would react. While the drugs were being administered, there were absolutely no side effects. It was as if Hayes was just a normal baby, hanging out in a hospital room. Those days were fun and relaxing. We took advantage of those days by cramming in physical and occupational therapy appointments. We also spent those days playing endless peekaboo, as it always made Hayes laugh out loud.

Things got more serious toward the eleventh day of each round. The mouth sores would begin and typically last for three days, along with fevers. By day eighteen, his white blood cells would begin showing signs of new production, as his bone marrow kicked into gear to reboost the system. White blood cells are responsible for healing the body, and that's exactly what they would do. It was amazing to see his body's natural reactions: once the white blood cell count started to rise, the mouth sores would go away.

On the nineteenth day we always grew anxious for the counts to reach the magical number that would allow us to take Hayes home. After only a few rounds, my mind would prepare for Hayes to come home so any setback in the round would set me off. I often grew impatient with the nurses and doctors around day nineteen.

We were told that most kids became weaker with each round. Their bodies would put up a good fight early on, and then begin to wear out. I feared this from the get-go, because the side effects were intense during the first round. The side effects on the second round didn't seem to be as intense, and Hayes's complexion was much better. Also, he was happier and seemed to be responding to the chemotherapy. But this was just an assumption until we actually got an MRI scan to verify.

As the second round of treatment was finishing, we were pleasantly surprised by the way Hayes handled it. His body seemed to be getting stronger and his energy level had picked up. We didn't just notice this ourselves, many of the nurses saw the physical changes in Hayes too. His coloring was much better and his eyes had their typical Hayes glow, compared to the first round when they were worn out with a sunken look. Hayes was playful and taking major strides during physical therapy. He was developmentally slower, but we were told that wasn't going to last his entire life. There was no neurological impairment, so it would just be a matter of time before he would catch up to his brother and sister.

Heath and Reese were in the crawling stages at this point, while Hayes was still learning to sit up consistently. In hindsight, that said a lot about how toxic the treatments were. There was a lot to be hopeful about because, while we watched his little body struggle to learn these things, his mind and spirit were amazing. Hayes would smile and laugh, even as his body was taking some serious abuse. He had the mentality of a prized fighter. His spirit was strong, resilient, and he carried a gritty determination. Hayes was never in a bad mood and never seemed to be depressed or unmotivated. He woke up each day with a smile on his face, ready to take on his next challenge.

Hayes sitting up in his crib while getting chemotherapy.

12

SCANXIETY

One of the most difficult things about chemotherapy is waiting for validation that treatments are working. The scans were done every three months, so we would sometimes go two or three rounds before having an MRI. While I got it that this was to avoid the additional radiation exposure, I'm a person who needs validation. I'll use a sports analogy to explain what this was like. I always hated two-a-day practices during the weeks that led up to our first game of the season. We were only practicing, so there was no way to determine if we were on the right path. How good were we, actually? When the first game approached, the nerves would settle into me but then be gone after the game. The games confirmed that our practice was paying off. In the same way, we thought the treatments were working, but that's just it, we only thought they were working. There was no validation until we had MRI results.

Waiting for MRI results were the most nerve-wracking experiences of our lives. I used to think I got nervous before a big game, but that wasn't comparable. Those results even beat the anxiety of being a freshman, straight out of high school, starting in my first-ever collegiate football game. It was in Baton Rouge, against the LSU Tigers. I walked out of the tunnel to see 93,000 people staring down at me. The opposing fans were leaning down to chant "Tiger Bait! Tiger Bait! Tiger Bait!" over and over again. It was a surreal experience.

So after almost sixty days and two rounds of chemo treatment, we were longing to be told it was working. The MRI consumed our every thought. In the cancer world, this is referred to as "scanxiety" because they are incredibly meaningful. You live and die by those results. They determined your path: either a long, enjoyable life or a life of dependency on toxic medication.

Scanxiety consumed us, particularly the first time around. All the signs seemed to be positive based on our amateur analysis, but we really had no idea. Yes, we were yearning for validation but, at the same time, we were dreading it for fear of negative results. I remember sitting at home with the older kids, just a few days before the MRI. We had just finished a prayer for positive results.

"Dad," Bo said, looking at me with tears in his eyes, "what if it doesn't work?"

"What if what doesn't work?" I replied, putting my arms around his shoulders.

"The treatment. What if the treatment doesn't work?" he asked as he wiped his eyes dry. The kids were feeling scanxiety too, and I didn't really have an answer for Bo. I had been wondering the same thing, to be honest. But Bo was relying on me for assurance and leadership.

"Then we will try something different," I said confidently, looking into his eyes. "We will do whatever it takes." I hugged all three kids in my arms that night. I had always had good relationships with my kids, but new levels of trust were developing as we knew that we needed each other. Love for each other was getting everyone through the stress of the treatments and the many what-if fears.

The love was multiplying inside our family, and also outside our family. March 12th was coming up. It was the triplets' first birthday, and we were planning a huge celebration. A key to staying positive throughout this journey was finding ways to celebrate, so we planned a party to celebrate their birthday with everyone who was standing behind us.

Hayes's Army was alive and strong and growing bigger each day. We had been planning a "Hayestough" 5K-walk event to raise awareness about childhood cancer and also to celebrate with all the strangers who had been concerned for our family. We invited everyone sharing this journey through social media. I thought a couple hundred people would come, and we designed T-shirts, stickers, and wristbands—all of which read "Hayestough." I was really excited about this upcoming event, so the planning was a needed distraction from the MRI we were about to have. Planning this event in honor of Hayes was therapeutic for us.

Finally, MRI day arrived, full of intense nerves and strong emotions. They had to sedate Hayes because it typically took two hours to get an accurate reading of both his brain and spine. Our hearts were beating hard and we felt uneasy as they wheeled him away. The MRI happened in the evening, so we wouldn't get results until the following day. They finished the scan around 8 p.m. Since it was late, and there was nothing really I could do, I decided to head home to be with the older kids while Savanna stayed overnight with Hayes.

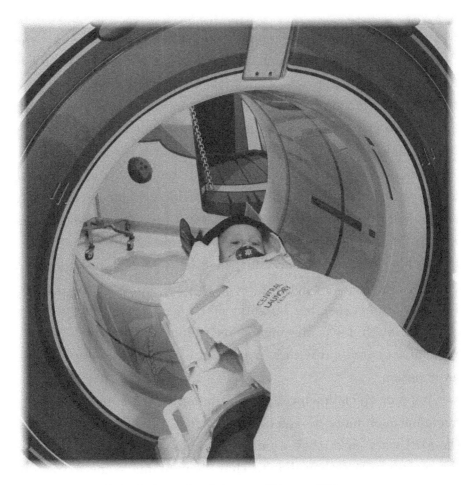

Hayes looks up at us during one of his many MRI exams.

That was an extremely long and lonely night for me as I lay in bed with no way of distracting my mind. I had become used to sleeping alone at that point, but this night was extremely quiet and depressing. I started missing the old days, when I would fall asleep next to Savanna. I missed my wife. I missed the normality of having someone to laugh with at bedtime. Savanna and I would often stay up until 1 or 2 a.m. just talking about random things. I have an excellent memory, and I love reminding Savanna of stupid little things that have happened in our lives together. It was my way to make her laugh. One night, I could sense that Savanna was dozing off. I hated it when she fell asleep before me. To wake her up, I started singing our junior-high fight song. Who remembers their junior high school's fight song? Well, apparently I do. And I felt like 1 a.m. on a Tuesday was the perfect time to bust it out. I'm tone-deaf, which made it even better.

"Hail, hail for Churchill Chargers, hail, hail for victory!" I sang it loudly and obnoxiously. Her eyes opened widely, immediately angry, as she had every right to be. I mean, what kind of husband wakes his wife in the middle of the night to reminisce? She was startled, but couldn't help it. She burst out laughing. Whether she laughed to make me feel good, or because I was actually funny, didn't matter. I didn't care because her laughter made me happy. I love making Savanna laugh. I was missing a moment like that, craving a classic, random conversation with her. Instead I just lay there in nervous anticipation.

At 4 p.m. the following day, we still hadn't heard any news. This made me even more nervous because I figured that, if results from the MRI were good, they would've come in to tell us first thing in the morning. But they didn't. That thought made me extremely uncomfortable. I sat next to Savanna and waited for any sign of a doctor. I would've been pacing, but I was worn out from pacing the entire morning. We both grew impatient and finally Savanna asked one of the nurses to page the oncologist and let her know we had been waiting all day for the results. It was inconsiderate.

"They obviously have no idea what it's like to wait for one of these things," I said to Savanna. It was true. I mean, I'm glad that they haven't experienced this because I wouldn't wish cancer on anyone, but they were definitely lacking empathy. The whole day was excruciating and emotional.

Hayes was sitting in his crib watching *Daniel Tiger's Neighborhood*. I made my way over to peek down at him, and then the door opened. It was our oncologist. I read her body language as she walked in the room. Her head was down, and there was a scowl in her eyes.

"Sit down," she recommended, and I made my way toward Savanna. I knew that was a bad sign. She took a deep breath and began the much-dreaded conversation. "There's not an easy way to tell you this," she could've stopped there. We knew what was next. "Unfortunately, it's not working. The tumor on his spine appears more advanced than it was in January. I'm so sorry."

She continued speaking, but nothing she said seemed to matter to us. Savanna began to cry. She had been so optimistic that things were going well—we both felt that way. Now we were completely devastated, our hopes erased by one conversation. Hopes that had taken two months to build up suddenly came crashing down again. I hugged Savanna as she cried in my arms. I was still shocked and confused. I felt angry, too angry to cry.

After taking a moment to ourselves, I looked up at the oncologist. "How can we put our son through that kind of hell only to be told it's not working?" I asked. She had no explanation that seemed appropriate for the moment. I knew she was doing her best to help Hayes, but my frustration grew as I thought of all the time and energy we had just spent trying to get Hayes better.

The 5K walk and birthday celebration couldn't have come at a better time. We had just been knocked down from this news, and we needed recharging. I was beginning to see just how volatile hope can be, and it needed to build back up again. We were only a few days from the 5K and the organization was amazing. We sent out word through our Instagram, Facebook, and Twitter accounts.

The birthday party was made even more important to our family after this devastating news. There was a thought in my head that I never shared with anyone, but I had a vivid impression that this could be the first and last birthday Hayes would have with us. It wasn't as though I was throwing in the towel, but the MRI result was making me understand just how serious his cancer was.

I was unable to sleep for a few days leading up to the 5K event. I was in a pretty dark place. My mind was taking me to extremely lonely places as I fought back thoughts of a future life without our angelic little boy. No matter how hard I tried to control my thoughts, I failed. It caused me to lose two consecutive nights of sleep. I was going on more than 48 hours without even a wink of sleep. I knew that I needed to be the rock for my family, that they were all looking to me for strength. So I visited my doctor to get a sleep aide. I was desperate to be able to function and start the hope buildup process all over again. I was prescribed some Ambien and took my first pill that night, which knocked me out. I woke up nine hours later expecting to feel optimistic and recharged. But that's not what I felt at all. I had hit rock bottom, and struggled to even get out of bed as tears flowed nonstop. I had never experienced this kind of low in my life—even the initial diagnosis wasn't as shocking to my system as this was. This darkness was taking over my entire body and mind.

When we first found the tumor, there had been a plan of attack: surgery was scheduled immediately, followed by chemo. We had been taking actions toward a positive outcome, so I didn't have time to feel depressed or knocked down. Each step helped me feel hope. But this week was different. There was nothing to do, no relief to help me escape the depression. I spent most of my waking hours sobbing uncontrollably, away from the kids and Savanna. I didn't want them to see me like that. Fortunately, I knew my body and mind extremely well, and sensed something was wrong with me. I felt chemically unstable.

I had spent a year in the pharmaceutical industry and was well-versed in it. I knew that certain drugs had extreme side effects, so I googled depression as a side effect of Ambien. Turned out it was known to bring out severe depression in moments of crisis, even leading to suicide. I immediately grabbed the bottle and tossed the remaining pills in the garbage. I knew it was the drug that was holding me down in an extremely dangerous place. A few days passed and I could feel my body responding. My energy picked back up and the depression began leaving my body. I could physically feel the Ambien leaving my system, which was just in time for the 5K event.

When we originally planned this 5K, our hope was to create awareness for Hayes and childhood cancer. Our intent was to foster light and hope in this moment of despair. I also wanted to thank everyone for the incredible support they were showing our family. I believe it's our purpose as humans to help each other in moments like this. Humanity is about picking each other up, and it's a duty to serve others in need.

We showed up that morning with all six kids, including Hayes. We had heard that several people intended to be there, but I never imagined the turnout we saw as we pulled up to the City of Holladay building. Easily 1,500 people had shown up that morning to lift us up. We felt overcome with extreme love. I have no doubt that this event was God's way of giving us the emotional boost we needed. The timing was not coincidental. Support was palpable as people came from all over Utah to show us that they were in this fight alongside us. There's a saying in the cancer community: "Nobody fights alone." On March 12, we had an entire army behind us to lift our spirits.

The streets were full of people sporting "Hayestough" T-shirts. Underneath the logo was the saying, "Tough times don't last, but tough people do." That was something my college coach, Kyle Whittingham, would say when things weren't going well. One time, he delivered that message after we lost a close game to Air Force. Everyone was down that week, so Coach Whittingham called a team meeting.

"You think this is hard?" he had asked. He stared directly into our eyes as he walked around us slowly. "You're all here, sitting down, feeling sorry for yourselves. And people are out there, in the real world, facing real problems. Your problems aren't real. You lost a football game! I can promise you that life will get much harder than this." He stopped talking and walked out of the room without saying another word. It was one of the most profound statements I had ever heard a coach say. He had a way of putting things into perspective. Little did I realize, I would find myself facing one of those real-world problems.

To say the 5K was incredibly successful would be an understatement. It was life changing. It inspired each of us and buoyed our spirits for the treatments that were ahead. Following the event, we immediately stopped feeling sorry for ourselves. It gave us a glimpse of just how big Hayes's Army was getting. So many people were there behind the scenes, fighting with us. They all had our backs as we waited to hear the next steps from the oncology team.

The team of physicians had spent the week discussing the appropriate plan for treating Hayes. We were still at home, enjoying life, recovering from the birthday celebrations. I was still cleaning up frosting from the "cake smash" the triplets did. That frosting was stuck in the hardwood floor for days. We were soaking up every minute with Hayes at home. Each piece of bad news made us more awareness of how precious life is. Although we had reasons to be depressed, that wasn't the life we wanted. Our older kids needed hope. From what I had experienced in the three days when Ambien took control of my body, I knew depression would lead me down a path of no return. So we exchanged our sadness and anxiety for joy. We focused on our love for Hayes and considered each additional day we had with him to be a gift.

Hayes seemed to be blessing us with his divine spirit and contagious smile. He had a way of making everything feel okay, even in the darkest moments. People would constantly say, "I don't know how you do it. I can't imagine the pain you are going through," or "I don't know what I would do if I was in your shoes." Well, they didn't have Hayes lifting them up every day. We soaked up the good that he sent out. He lifted our spirits, and part of me felt he was the one guiding us through every decision. It was his mighty spirit that pushed us to make the best decisions, regardless of what the doctors said.

The doctors wanted to abandon the entire protocol that we had committed to completing, a protocol that had been proven. We felt uneasy because it was the main reason we had decided to treat Hayes at Primary Children's Hospital. This protocol was aggressive and we believed in it, so we felt extremely uncomfortable with their decision to change the direction of his treatment. They proposed an at-home protocol. It would allow Hayes to be with his loved ones as we gave him chemotherapy in our house. It meant that Savanna and I would be together, which we both missed so much. There was no question of the appeal, from a personal standpoint.

I was overwhelmed with the amount of duties on my plate. I had become exhausted and being away from Savanna was taking a toll on me. And Savanna missed the kids. Although she was coming home each night for a few hours, she had been missing some big developmental stages as Heath and Reese began to crawl and stand on their own. We spent nights talking at length about this new protocol, and wrote down the pros and cons of each option. We rehashed this list often, and determined to continue following our intuitions and promptings.

Savanna also turned to her Facebook support group for advice, as there were other parents who had been in our shoes. One of the moms insisted Savanna reach out to a doctor in Cincinnati, a specialist on this particular type of cancer, who even authored the Head Start II protocol we had been following. Savanna was able to find his email address, and followed an instinct to reach out to him blindly. Only forty-five minutes later, she received a response from him. He shared our concern about changing the protocol prematurely, and agreed to look at the recent MRIs and review Hayes's medical history.

Savanna called me immediately. I was excited by the passion in her voice, as it had been a while since I had heard her exude that much energy. This gave us an extreme amount of hope. We had learned over the past few months that physicians don't have all the answers, and that each one has a different belief about what's best. So seeking a second opinion was necessary.

Meanwhile, we weren't gonna miss out on an opportunity to create some memories. We were craving a family getaway, it happened to be spring break, and Bo was playing in a major baseball tournament. So we loaded up the car and set off for a weekend in St. George, Utah. While on vacation, we received an email from the physician in Cincinnati. He had a recommendation:

"We have reviewed your particular case and met as a team. We feel it is extremely premature to abandon this protocol. In our experience, this treatment can take several rounds before results are seen on MRI. I advise you to stay the course, and I am willing to discuss this in detail with your oncology team."

We were thrilled to receive that email because it reaffirmed the direction Savanna and I were already leaning towards. Our list of pros for the proposed at-home protocol was filled with things that benefitted Savanna and I, and perhaps the other children. They fulfilled our needs—not Hayes's. This was his journey, his fight, and we felt his needs should be our needs. So we decided to go against our oncologist's recommendation and stick with the protocol that would require four more rounds of chemotherapy.

The physicians at Primary Children's Hospital hesitated to continue it because they feared Hayes's body wouldn't be able to handle the intensity. We knew our son much better than they did, and we knew what he could handle. Hayes was tough, extremely resilient, and was only getting stronger. We had made our decision and weren't looking back.

The Tate family just prior to the Hayestough 5k walk.

13

ALTERNATIVE MEDICINE

the next four months called on the entire family to sacrifice something, but all we cared about was Hayes and getting him better. During the next rounds, we researched ways to improve Hayes's quality of life. Many people had sent us articles on alternative medicines known to treat cancer. I was always skeptical, but I read many articles that included everything from frankincense to natural oils. I weeded out a lot of them.

One treatment that was extremely intriguing was cannabis oil, also known as CBD hemp oil. I didn't have much knowledge, personal experience, or stance on it. But I had never witnessed a loved one suffer through pain or sickness before, either. We studied up and found that the positive outweighed the negative. Savanna had been researching this alternative approach for quite some time, and eventually sold me on trying it to improve Hayes's life during this battle with brain cancer.

Cannabis oil had been known to suppress nausea, increase social interaction, and calm the nerves. Articles discussed successes with brain tumors: there had been tests in lab rats that showed it to suffocate cancer cells and shrink brain tumors. At this point, any research showing a way to reduce tumor mass was music to our ears. We were willing to attempt any form of therapy. At the very least, we were educating ourselves on every possible approach, which is what parents need to do as advocates.

One afternoon, Savanna and I were out for a walk. We joked about how we would go about getting cannabis oil to explore this alternative approach. "How does one even get access to something like that?" Savanna asked.

"Too bad we don't have any connections," I replied. I then painted the picture of a Mormon couple with six kids in a Suburban driving into a sketchy neighborhood looking for some weed. "Um, excuse me sir," I said, mocking some dorky, out-of-touch man with cargo pants pulled up to his ribs. I acted it out to make Savanna laugh. "I'm interested in getting some of that marijuana, ya know, the Mary Jane, as the kids say nowadays." I winked and gave Savanna a nudge. This was exactly what I envisioned in my head as we played with the idea of giving Hayes some medical marijuana.

As I was playing out this scenario with Savanna on our walk around the neighborhood, I got a friend request on Facebook from an old football buddy. I will go ahead and call him Jeremy. I hadn't seen or heard from Jeremy in fifteen years. I felt it was odd that he was requesting to be my friend, not because of the years that had passed since we had touched base, but because Jeremy happened to be the guy who had supplied many of the stoners with weed.

It was an ironic moment. I accepted the friend request and continued the walk toward home. When we got inside, an alert on my phone let me know I had a private Facebook message from Jeremy. I wasted no time opening it.

"Hey Steve, it's Jeremy. I know it's been a while and I'm sure you are wondering why I am messaging you out of the blue. But I felt like I needed to reach out to you concerning your boy. I am so sorry to hear of his recent diagnosis and noticed he had been spending lots of time at the hospital on chemotherapy. I want to offer my support and hopefully act as a resource for an alternative approach for your boy. I live in California and sell medicinal marijuana to doctors, and felt like it could benefit Hayes. Here is my cell phone number. Please reach out to me if I can help out in any way."

My jaw dropped. *What are the odds?* I thought. I called out to Savanna and tossed her my phone. She read the message and her facial expression was priceless. Her eyes were widening with each sentence she processed.

"Shut up!" she said as she pushed my shoulder in disbelief. It was a classic Savanna response and a very good impression of Elaine from Seinfeld. "What are the odds?" she asked.

I wasted no time calling Jeremy to get all the information I could about his personal experience with medicinal marijuana for children fighting cancer. He had an incredible wealth of knowledge that was enlightening to hear. I was a little hesitant, to be honest, wondering what was in it for him. We talked for almost an hour and I began to realize he was only reaching out as a concerned friend who wanted to help in any way possible. He refused to accept payment for any of it. The hesitation I had was erased and I agreed to try it with Hayes. I knew it couldn't be worse than the morphine drips they gave him for mouth sores. The morphine was extremely addictive and we regularly had to ween him off the narcotics. In addition, it was giving him additional side effects, like an extremely itchy face. I was willing to try an alternative approach and so was Savanna. Our main focus was helping Hayes.

If you would've told me in high school that Jeremy was going to be in my life fifteen years later, offering love and support by providing me with medicinal marijuana, I probably would've punched you in the face in disbelief. *What had happened to my boring life?* I thought.

Only a few days following our conversation, we put a small dose on one of Hayes's dissolvable teething tablets and stuck it in his cheek. It smelled like a skunk, almost unbearably so, and that caused us to be extremely nervous as we tried to be discreet since medicinal CBD was still not legal in Utah. We did this twice a day for his entire treatment.

There was a noticeable difference. He was much more engaged with us and playful. His energy levels were substantially higher when he was taking it. I noticed a healthier coloring in his face, and it seemed to suppress nausea during the days when he was experiencing side effects. Even the nurses commented on the differences they noticed. Many of them couldn't believe how good he looked. His physical appearance was livelier, his interactions were more social and jovial, and he was putting on weight from having the munchies. Not joking. His appetite increased significantly. The rounds in which we used CBD were much better than the rounds without it. We were becoming big believers, from a quality of life standpoint.

We both felt a need to make sure we did everything possible for our little boy. It's amazing what lengths you are willing to go to when your loved one is ill. Initially, I was extremely hesitant to include this chapter for fear of backlash. But I feel strongly about sharing something that helped a child whose odds weren't favorable when it came to winning this battle against an evil disease. I don't want to create controversy, but I do want to give you an idea of the approach we took to improve his quality of life and possibly cure him of cancer. If you haven't faced a similar situation, it's my hope that you can find sympathy for our decision. I felt a need to do anything and everything so that Hayes would be with me throughout my entire life.

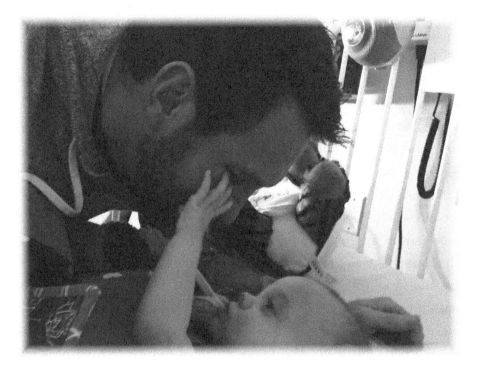

I look into Hayes's eyes while the side effects kick in.

14

VALIDATION

We were deep into the next rounds of treatments and the seasons were changing. We had begun this journey in the heart of winter, during dark and gloomy days that were cold and snowy. As summer approached, it seemed the seasons were hand in hand with the journey we were facing. What started off as depressing and hopeless in January, had developed into more hope and joy as we advanced through the calendar year.

Hayes was getting chubbier and thriving during his chemotherapy treatments. His cheeks were even starting to resemble Heath's. We were also shaving Heath's head frequently to make sure that Hayes knew his brother had his back. In fact, all the boys in the house were sporting shaved heads. Except for me. I'm too much of a pretty boy to shave my head. And I needed something to take attention away from the dark circles that were permanently around my eyes. A shaved head, combined with the dark-black circles, would have made me look like Uncle Fester from *The Addam's Family*. I told you I still had a little pride left, right? It was a no-go on the shaved head, but don't worry, I had a nice discussion with Hayes and he totally understood.

The kids were insanely busy with their activities. Bo was playing baseball, and sometimes had four games a week. It served as a great distraction for both of us, as we both enjoyed it. I spent many hours throwing baseballs in the backyard with Wes and Bo. It was a major stress reliever for all of us and created a father-and-sons bond. Bo was excelling at baseball. During the season's opening game, Bo took a fastball sent right down the middle of the plate and knocked it over the fence. I was so happy for him as I watched him circle the bases with a giant grin on his face. It was one of several homeruns that he was to hit that season.

Mia was also doing well with ballet and gymnastics, in addition to being the socialite that she is. She's always been an incredible older sister. She spent many days playing with her siblings and caring for them. She was born with maternal instincts and, in some ways, she was filling a little bit of a void when Savanna couldn't be at the house.

Wes was playing soccer for the first time. He's a natural athlete and was thriving in this new activity, often scoring multiple goals during games. Wes was in preschool three afternoons a week. He was also spending time with me and Bo in the backyard, learning to swing the bat and throw the ball around.

The babies were walking, and they were extremely busy doing it. We spent most days chasing them around the house and cleaning up boxes of spilled cereal. Our house was typically messy. I've seen cleaner homes at fraternities.

Things were extremely chaotic at our house, but it was therapeutic and exactly what we needed. Each night consisted of some sort of game or recital. The kids were giving us life, giving up plenty of reasons to be happy. We were focused on each of them and their needs, so we didn't have time to sulk from our ongoing fight at the hospital.

Savanna and I weren't getting much time together, other than casual hugs and kisses when we exchanged roles around 4 p.m. each day. Occasionally Savanna would come to the hospital after the babies were in bed, leaving Bo in charge for an hour or so. We spent those times just hanging out with each other and talking. We savored every moment we had together. Our love was strong, and it felt as though we were closer than ever, which seemed odd because it had been a long time since we had been intimate. And by intimate, I mean sexual. Sorry Mom and Dad, I know this is something that we never talk about in our family, but how do you think we ended up with six kids? To avoid discomfort, you could skip the next paragraph.

Without any time or opportunity to be intimate, I felt like I was in high school again. Sometimes we went several weeks without sex, which might not seem all that long for some couples, but it wasn't normal for us. Sex was good for my health and my psyche, and I needed to relieve the some of that stress. We both needed it, but we seriously lacked the privacy—until we found a bathroom that had a mobile hospital bed in it. Yep, a random bathroom that just so happened to have a bed in it. It was a Godsend for the two of us. We were extremely strategic about how both of us found our way into the bathroom. It was like scene from *Grey's Anatomy*. We were quick and to the point, but this is something that we both needed, and that our relationship needed. We made trips to the bathroom several times a week.

It's common for couples to part ways during stressful times like this. In fact, divorce rates were extremely high in the Facebook support groups—sometimes greater than 60 percent. I never felt like we were going to be part of that percentage, not even for a moment. We had a great relationship, similar to Chip and Joanna Gaines from *Fixer Upper*. (Yeah, I watch that show like the rest of the world. I actually enjoy decorating and fixing things up. There—I said it. It feels good to get that off my chest. Man, I never imagined this book would become my own little therapist and confessional.) Our relationship has always been centered on friendship. We have an obvious attraction to each other and our chemistry is radiant, but we love making each other laugh. We tend to balance each other out in stressful times, which helped us cope with this current trial.

Hayes was continuing to touch the lives of everyone who came in contact with him at the hospital. We were told that many of the nurses were requesting to care for Hayes during their shifts. During treatments, they were required to take his vitals every few hours. And there were times when, in the middle of the night, Hayes would wake up as they were taking his temperature. He would turn to them, smile, and engage in a game of peekaboo while laughing with the nurses. It wasn't typical behavior. The nurses were used to babies crying when woken up in the middle of the night. But Hayes was always excited to see them, even if it was 3 a.m. Those nurses were part of Hayes's Army and the love went both ways.

The hospital has an entire support staff, and we became extremely familiar with it. All were pretty much focused on making us feel comfortable and giving us any additional support we needed. They worked as a fluid unit for the most part, but there were moments that we didn't want to see certain people that came to visit. It was nothing against them personally, but the hospital had certain people assigned to us that tended to make things awkward for Savanna and I. We craved our privacy, and having additional people in our little room was annoying.

Primary Children's Hospital has volunteer chaplains who are are assigned to provide moral and social support for patients and their families. It's definitely a great concept and we appreciated it at times. There was a certain chaplain who would come to check on us every day. She always asked the same questions: "How are you?" and "How are your other kids?"

It took everything in my power not to respond, "Hey lady, I hardly know you and you expect me to spill my guts to you? I don't even talk to my parents about my issues, yet you are somehow going to have the magic key to open this messed-up vault in my head?"

One of the reasons we shared our story with the world on social media was to avoid having to tell the story to every single person who inquired. Social media was also becoming my journal, a place where I could write out my emotions. To me, this was much more effective than conversing with a random chaplain. I dreaded her arrival. One time I saw her face through the window and hurried to duck my head into a pillow. When the door slowly opened, I pretended to be asleep. I know she meant well, but I needed my space and so did Savanna.

In fact, we were both craving personal time. We often daydreamed about yanking the cords off Hayes and running away with the kids. There was something appealing about going to a place where we knew nobody, to start a new life. Like a small town in Texas where I could coach high school football, and we could live on a ranch. I was probably watching too much *Fixer Upper*, because small towns in Texas were becoming extremely appealing. This new life would of course include Hayes's perfect health.

The daydreaming was a distraction from reality, and we turned to it quite often—especially with the second MRI approaching. Scanxiety was taking over again. Mentally, we again observed every single aspect of Hayes and convinced ourselves that it was all working. He did look and act very healthy.

Savanna and I didn't talk about this second MRI often, because there was nothing either of us could say or do that would ease the stress and anxiety. Other people would try to calm us down by relating some personal story. Typically, their tale had very little relevance to our situation. I think that people generally didn't know what to say. But they felt an obligation to empathize. So they dug deep into their personal experience logbook and tried to tie in something tragic or nerve-wracking that happened to them, even if it had zero relevance. I could write a book on what not to say to people who are going through a crisis. I didn't need pep talks. I didn't need to hear, "Everything happens for a reason" nor "We are never given more than we can handle." *Really?* Because I was pretty sure I had been given more than I could handle. And I definitely didn't need to hear about how hard it was watching your dog suffer while recovering from cataract surgery. All I wanted to hear from people was that things were going to be okay. That's it, very simple. Just tell me "It's going to be okay" and move on.

I talked about this with Savanna in the MRI waiting room, and she felt the same way. Now, as we all know too well, sometimes things don't work out the way we want them to. But even after disappointing results, life has a way of working itself out. And in the end, things are okay. All we had been through in the past year was evidence of that truth. We were still ticking, weren't we?

I repeated this in my head the entire time Hayes was in radiology getting his second MRI. I was convincing myself that things were going to be okay, even though I was still scared out of my mind. We felt more pressure this time, since the treatment path was one that Savanna and I chose. We had gone against the doctor's advice, so it was all on us. All we could do was hope that the MRI showed our intuitions to be right once again. We were waiting for validation.

This MRI happened early in the day, so we were hoping for results in a timely manner. Nerves were controlling our every thought, and there's no way I could've handled the anxiety for more than a few hours—especially not overnight. A physician came in to check on Hayes before she left for the day. This wasn't our typical oncologist, but she was extremely friendly. As she was about to leave our room, as if the thought had come to her abruptly, she asked, "Hey, do you want me to go read the MRI?"

"Uh, yes. If you have them already," Savanna replied anxiously.

"I think we do, I'll be right back," she said with a casual manner and left the room. Her casualness calmed me. It was if she was letting me know things would be okay.

I stood and paced around the room like a caged tiger. Savanna remained seated on the hospital bed with her knees bent against her chest. We were silent. Even Hayes was silent, fascinated with some dot he had found on his shirt, but I think he was also feeling the anticipation. The room felt heavy with anxiety.

"What if we were wrong?" I suddenly asked Savanna. "What if we made the wrong decision by sticking with this protocol?"

"We went with how we felt," Savanna replied with a casual, matter-of-fact tone. "And it hasn't faulted us yet." she added confidently.

The door opened. "Guys...it's awesome!" the doctor exclaimed.

Excitement shot through my entire body. It was one of the best feelings of my entire existence. Joy filled the hospital room and our eyes filled with tears of relief. We had finally received the validation we needed.

"What do you mean by 'awesome?'" Savanna asked curiously, with a gigantic grin on her face. The physician turned to the computer and pulled up the report. Typically I hate looking at images, but not now. I was staring at that computer screen with full attention.

"It looks really good, guys. Everything has seemed to clear up since the last MRI scan." She made one final assessment of the report: "There's a little residual in his lower spine, but this is extremely positive." We could see the excitement in her eyes.

The next couple of weeks were some of the best weeks of our lives. We felt like we had been given another gift, similar to the time after the initial surgery that removed the tumor. There were no bands of doubt holding us down, and we were experiencing a sense of freedom. A new life.

While Hayes was home recovering from this round of treatment, I felt the need to book a trip. In fact, I felt the need to book a couple of trips: one to Disneyland and one to Hawaii in February of 2017. One thing this experience had taught me was not wait for the "right time." Before, I would've hesitated and avoided it because perhaps we didn't have the "time" or it was "too expensive." I would make excuses—but not anymore. Our lives had just been put on pause for six months. So I was committed to enjoying life with my family and fulfilling my promise to the kids. I wasn't about to ask for permission from the oncology team. Our family needed a vacation, a time to be together without doctors or nurses, when we could enjoy Hayes.

I reserved a condo in Newport Beach, CA for two weeks before Thanksgiving. It felt really good to do, therapeutic even, because it wasn't typical "Steve Tate" behavior. The old me would've dragged my feet or made some stupid excuse, but I had learned how valuable each moment with my family is. Booking that trip marked an extremely big step for me and my family. It was a moment I never thought would come in January or even in March when we got the discouraging MRI results. Things looked so different in June: I wasn't allowing the what-if fears to control my decisions and I was high from positive scan results, so nothing was going to get in the way of creating much-needed, happy memories at Disneyland. It also showed how much I had changed, given that after we found out we were having triplets, thoughts of Disneyland had caused my first-ever panic attack.

We still had one more round to go, which was the stem-cell transplant. It's a procedure used to reset the entire body, similar to a bone-marrow transplant, except it uses a body's own cells rather than a donor's. In the first round of chemotherapy, they had spent almost nine hours taking Hayes's stem cells from his own body to prepare for this final stage of treatment. This procedure is common with extremely aggressive types of cancer, as it provides a means to kill off any remaining cancer cells. Nothing in the cancer world is guaranteed, but the chance of relapse shrinks considerably.

We had been warned that it was an extremely intense form of treatment, and that Hayes would get really sick—much sicker than any of the previous rounds. I was a little apprehensive about this last step, but I also wanted to make sure that we didn't have any regrets in the future.

When I face a critical decision like this, I try to look forward as if reflecting back by asking "Would my future self regret not doing it?" I knew that taking this aggressive approach would leave me with the least amount of regret if Hayes ever relapsed. Throughout my life, I have found that regrets usually occur when you fail to do something difficult. The easier approach is usually the one we choose because it doesn't require a lot of mental fortitude and perhaps doesn't challenge us physically. Choosing the difficult path for my son, knowing he would get even sicker, was one of the harder things I have had to do as a parent. During this journey, we were continually faced with extreme decisions about putting our little boy through some sort of pain. But we knew that for Hayes to live a long life, we needed to take the hard route.

Heath, Hayes, and Reese with Savanna on Mother's Day.

15

ONE LAST HURDLE

"We can do this," Savanna said to me as we walked into the hospital for the final stage of Hayes's therapy. I needed the reassurance because I was extremely apprehensive. I had heard from several parents, whose children had stem-cell transplants, that the treatment was harder on their children than I had thought. The stories terrified me. I knew there wasn't an alternative, but still I feared for Hayes's health and safety.

"My son got so sick," one mother wrote in an Instagram message, "that they had to move him to the ICU four times." This particular mom would check in on us every once in a while, via social media. Her son also had a brain tumor. Our number of social-media followers had been growing rapidly. We had an array of audiences, and only a small fraction had been directly impacted by childhood cancer. The majority had simply taken an interest in Hayes, drawn in by his angelic appearance and smile.

"Only four more weeks," Savanna said, continuing her pep talk. "Look how far we've come." We had endured five rounds of treatment. We had come far, and while I was excited to be on the last step, it was a giant step. It involved a beast of a treatment that was going to take our son to the edge of death. It was much more than what he had already been through.

During stem-cell transplants they use extremely high dosages of chemotherapy to kill off the bone marrow entirely. Then, after the bone marrow is destroyed, they perform the "stem-cell rescue," as they often referred to it. They used the term "rescue" because that's exactly what they were doing: rescuing the body before it shuts down completely.

The schedule was similar to our previous rounds. The only differences were the amount of chemotherapy (which would intensify his usual side effects) and one additional drug that they hadn't used before. Its extreme toxicity would require us to give Hayes a bath every few hours because if it stayed on his body, it would burn his skin. They planned on observing his mouth sores closely and give him morphine around the clock to provide some relief until the white blood cells grew back. Some kids had been known to pass out from mouth sores, as an airway can become swollen and eventually close up.

The first week was similar to our other rounds. I would arrive for my afternoon shift, and Hayes was happy and playful. I loved taking him out of his crib, holding him on my lap, and bouncing him up and down. He loved it when I threw him up in the air. I tossed him more cautiously than I did the other babies, but he would laugh so hard. Hayes was soaking up our time together and I got the feeling that he was living each day as a gift. Although he couldn't express his emotions with words, Hayes's spirit let us know. Our souls were connected. In some ways, he was easier to communicate with than our other kids.

The mouth sores showed up around day ten, and stayed much longer. I could see in Hayes's eyes that he didn't feel well, which was excruciating to witness. He was throwing up way more than the other rounds as well. I constantly tried to take his attention off the pain with toys or television shows. *Daniel Tiger's Neighborhood* seemed to be the only thing that distracted Hayes, so we spent endless hours watching it. In one episode, Daniel Tiger had to go to the doctor because he was sick. I began imaging what was going on in Hayes's head while watching this show. "Hey, Daniel quit your whining," he would say from his lonely hospital room with four cords attached to him and mouth sores lining his throat.

There were many times when I wondered whether Hayes knew he was sick. *Does he have any idea that he is battling a life-threatening disease?* I would search for any possible sign of an answer to this question, but I never came up with a definite answer. I never saw him act frustrated when he couldn't do something, or jealous of his brother and sister playing around him. In fact, it was quite the opposite. He loved watching them have fun as they played with toys and had temper tantrums.

Hayes never once had a temper tantrum—it just wasn't in him. He was never sad and I never felt as though Hayes was depressed about his condition. I sensed that Hayes simply didn't compare himself to the other babies, because he didn't need to in some weird way. His joys in life were much different than theirs. Toys and gadgets weren't what made Hayes happy, like most toddlers. Hayes found joy in other people, in other babies. He enjoyed connecting, and he did it through his eyes. I have ever met anyone with such powerful eyes. He found happiness by making other people happy and then watching them laugh. His eyes would become fixated on your eyes until you smiled or acknowledged him, and then he would immediately smile or laugh in return.

I witnessed this vividly, just before the stem-cell transplant began, when the babies received a ball-bopping machine. It would toss little plastic balls in the air while playing a song. The balls would go in the machine and then be spit up in the air for a brief moment, before going right back in again. Hayes sat on the floor observing his brother and sister as they pushed the button that released the balls. Heath and Reese laughed so hard at seeing those balls fly in and out of the machine. Hayes enjoyed it too, but not from the same source as his brother and sister. Hayes certainly liked the music and movement, but he was much more focused on his siblings. He would laugh when they laughed. And as he watched them run around him chasing balls that had gone astray, he began clapping, much more entertained by seeing them happy than by the toy.

Hayes's definition of happiness was different, noticeably so because I had two others to compare him to. He oozed a selfless love. I always got the feeling that he was much more concerned about the people around him than he was about himself.

On July 8, 2016, Hayes received his stem-cell transplant. In the cancer world, this is considered a new birthday. The entire fourth floor came into our room to sing "Happy Birthday" to him, exchanging the word "birthday" for "bone-marrow transplant day." They made it a really special day for Hayes, a day to celebrate for many years to come. In some ways, they were right—it was a special day. But we were already celebrating each and every day that we had. I wasn't planning on celebrating bone-marrow transplant day in the future, to be honest, because it would imply we had forgotten that each day is a gift.

Hayes was deathly ill for about a week. The fevers came every day, and vomiting was frequent. He battled nausea constantly, and had no desire to do anything other than sleep. Fortunately, he never had to be transferred to ICU, but his body was taking a beating. His eyes were sunken and sad. His energy was nonexistent. At one point, he didn't have the energy or tolerance for food so he was fed intravenously. It seemed barbaric, to be honest, but cancer treatment in general is barbaric. There just isn't an easy way to treat this beast of a disease. The only thing that got me through that week, full of sorrow and sickness, was the light promised at the end of the tunnel. I could finally see that light, and I would often cling to it during those dark days filled with extreme side effects.

They measured his blood count each day to observe when the new blood cells were coming in. By day twenty-four, I could sense that Hayes's energy level was picking up and that he was beginning to feel better. His counts were picking up and the mouth sores slowly began to disappear. There was no more saliva surrounding his pillow, and he was starting to show signs of being himself. It was extremely rewarding to watch this because it represented the beginning of the end. I knew this chapter was close to fading and our new post-treatment life was about to begin.

The physicians were cautious with Hayes, almost too cautious in my opinion. We had done five previous rounds in the hospital, so we knew the routine. Even ten days after white blood cells began showing up in Hayes's lab work, the doctors had no intention of sending him home. It was extremely irritating for me and Savanna, as our patience was wearing thin so close to the end. Each day they would push going home off further without a good explanation. I wanted my son home with the rest of the family. I was sick of the hospital and the physicians.

I finally hit my limit after three days and "angry Steve" kicked into gear. One morning I asked for the nurse to page the physician. I wanted a reasonable explanation for keeping Hayes at the hospital. His white blood cell count was exactly where it needed to be. His mannerisms were good and his activity level was back to old form. Hayes was feeling well and we were wasting time at the hospital. He could be at home with his siblings, who he hadn't seen in a very long time. This stem-cell phase had been going on twenty-eight days. We had totaled 120 overnight stays in this hospital, and I was ready to never see it again.

"Did you page me?" the doctor asked as he made his way into the room with two other physicians at his side.

I tried my best to remain calm. "I want to know why Hayes isn't home already. I want a reasonable explanation for why you haven't released him yet." I could tell, by the expression in the doctor's face, that I had stuck a nerve. He was turning red.

"Your son isn't going home any time soon," he replied in an arrogant manner. I could tell that he felt I was questioning his authority. "There is no way he will be discharged within the next few days," he stated defensively with no elaboration or explanation.

"Why?" I asked. "I want an explanation. If there is something preventing him from leaving, I want a plan of action in front of me so that we can get him home." I could tell the doctor's blood was boiling and that his pride wasn't going to allow someone to question his medical decision. But I didn't care, so I continued. "I have spent 120 days in this hospital by my son's side and I have observed his every action. You observed him for maybe three days, and I feel you're making a decision based on what is best for you and not necessarily what is best for Hayes and our family." My tone was sharp and direct.

I knew what was going on. During my days as a medical device rep, I studied healthcare enough to know everything that physicians based decisions on. And a major influencer was the fear of readmission. A physician and a hospital are actually punished if a patient goes home and returns to the hospital days later, sometimes monetarily. Readmissions are considered really negative things in the medical world. I knew that this was motivating the doctor's decision, and I wasn't appreciative.

"I don't care about your readmission grades or track records. I'm taking him home," I insisted. Savanna stood next to me, staring at the ground. She hated controversy, so this was extremely uncomfortable for her. She never questioned doctors and, if some physician told her we couldn't take Hayes home for the remainder of the year, I think Savanna would just go with it. I say this half-jokingly, because she wanted him home. But she was also extremely easy-going and trusted physicians' decisions. Fortunately for me, I knew the ins and outs of the medical world and knew that it is run as a business. And this physician was more focused on his annual review than on our family and Hayes.

"We will see about that," he said, staring into my eyes. I'm surprised laser beams didn't come flying at me with that deathly stare. It was intense, but I didn't care. I stared right back at him and his cronies. I stood behind what I said.

The discharge papers were filled out that afternoon. And Hayes came home the next morning!

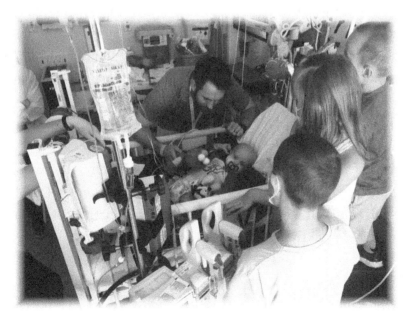

Hayes receives his stem-cell transplant while the family cheers him on.

16

THE GOLDEN BELL

July 23, 2016, was our day of independence. The discharge paperwork had been completed and Hayes was coming home. There was a sense of completion to our six-month fight—what an accomplishment! It almost didn't seem real. We had envisioned this day for so long and the fact that it had actually arrived was hard to comprehend. The day was beautiful, with not a cloud in the sky—the exact opposite from the morning on January 7 when Hayes had been diagnosed. January was cold, gray, and depressing, while this day was warm, bright, and full of hope. It was fitting for this milestone as we prepared to take Hayes home from the hospital, one final time. This was the beginning of a new chapter in our family's life.

The first thing we did to celebrate was to ring the golden bell. In the cancer world, whenever people finish their therapy, they celebrate with loved ones through this ceremony. It involves a song, and then the patient swings the bell. At Primary Children's Hospital, that bell was in the hallway on the fourth floor. Attached to it was a plaque that read:

Ring this bell
Three times well
It's toll to clearly say

My treatment's done
This course is run
And I am on my way!

During Hayes's treatment, I would walk by that bell every day and read the plaque. It represented a new life: one that didn't require bags of dripping chemotherapy medicine. From day one, the bell represented what we were working toward. To me, surviving cancer wasn't about life and death, it was about battling through every moment and fighting despite any odds. As I watched Hayes do just that, there were many moments when I would sit in the hospital room and wonder if he would make it to that special day. Sometimes things were so touch and go that it seemed like a pipe dream, a unicorn. I would often sit and daydream that we were watching Hayes ring the bell.

I knew that the golden bell didn't mean a life free from cancer. It didn't mean that you had been cured, or that your worries would be no more. That bell symbolized hope and freedom. It was a trophy for every child who had to endure endless hours of pain and torment, physically and mentally. It was an acknowledgment of that hardship and how they pressed forward, even if the odds weren't in their favor. That was how you earned your stripes as a cancer survivor.

The bell ceremony was one final gratification. The kids, whose innocence has been ripped from them, get to punch cancer in the ugly face one last time before moving on with their lives.

Since the bell was in the common hall leading to the hospital rooms, we regularly overheard family and friends celebrating. One March afternoon, I said to Savanna, "I am so happy for these kids and families, but I'm also so jealous of them. Will that ever be us?" I asked, searching for reassurance. I turned to look at her and noticed tears falling down her cheek. Hayes was taking one of his usual naps, so the room was silent, and the cheers and claps from outside filled it. I wanted to switch places with everyone in the hall that day. At that time, we had so many rounds remaining that we had to learn to live each day, hour by hour. So it was overwhelming to let our minds wander too far ahead. Don't get me wrong, our bell ceremony was something we envisioned would be the most magical day of our lives. But surviving the next 24-hours had been daunting and unimaginable enough.

After a week at home, on August 1, 2016, we were actually going to ring that bell. Walking back into the hospital was much more difficult than I anticipated. Savanna and I were definitely suffering from PTSD, which is common for cancer fighters and family members. We hadn't been officially diagnosed, but the symptoms were there, and they threatened to consume us at any given moment. I held Hayes and walked down the halls on the fourth floor. Those same halls that we had just left, where there had been happy times and sad times. I thought about the time I had taken Hayes for a wagon ride, one that will forever be engraved in my brain.

He was extremely sick that day, but I was determined to get him out of his crib to let him feel like a boy. I felt so sorry that Hayes couldn't enjoy some of those simple things that little babies should enjoy. I loaded him in a red wagon and attached the IV pole that was still administering his chemotherapy. He was so sick that his little body couldn't even sit up in the wagon, but that wasn't holding me back from giving my son some much-needed entertainment. I lined the wagon with pillows and warm blankets, and laid him down. He was confused at first and perhaps not in the mood, but I needed to do it to give him a simple experience that might take his mind off things. I began pulling him around the entire floor of the hospital, up and down the same hallway for an hour. His eyes grew a few centimeters that day, filling up with amazement. He was so happy to be out of his hospital room. His smile was big and his joy was obvious from the way he looked from side to side, not wanting to miss a single moment.

It was a flash flood of memories as we made our way down that hallway, on an August afternoon, to ring the golden bell. We had invited family and loved ones, and everyone was wearing their "Hayestough" T-shirts. There were camera crews surrounding us from the local news station. They had also been drawn to our story and had become part of Hayes's Army. Everyone gathered around the bell as Savanna held Hayes, and I felt a need to say something. I thanked our family and our friends. I thanked the physicians and staff.

"We love you, but we hope we don't ever come back," I said with a slight smirk on my face. The hallway filled with laughter.

We sang a song in unison, and then it was our cue to ring the golden bell. Savanna held Hayes as I took his little hand and helped him pull the rope. We pulled hard on that bell and swung it back and forth with complete pride.

I was so proud of Hayes in that moment. Never had I felt so proud in all my life. He had just conquered one of life's biggest challenges.

As we finished ringing the bell, I turned to thank everyone for coming. But Hayes fought to turn back toward the bell. He was still relearning some of his basic occupational skills and his hand-eye coordination was a work in progress, to say the least, but not in this moment. He reached his right hand around me and grasped that rope. Without any hesitation or need for assistance, Hayes swung the bell for a second time.

It was as if he knew what he had just accomplished and wanted to savor every opportunity to ring that bell. He swung it with so much joy, not just for the sound it made, but because of what it represented. I felt that Hayes had also been dreaming of this day for the past six months also. He was proud of himself, just as we were proud of him. I also believe that Hayes saw how happy we were as we rang the bell, and wasn't about to stop at one opportunity to see us so joyous. It was his way of communicating that he loved us.

Afterward, I made small talk with the people who came to support us. My eyes looked around the room to see everyone who had come that day, and they immediately landed on our oncologist. She stood in the back with a blank stare, almost emotionless. I thought, *What's her problem?* But there was a part of me that knew she had seen so many of these bell ceremonies, and understood the challenges that remained.

I knew that day that Hayes wasn't cured, or cancer-free, but this ceremony wasn't about that anyway. Ringing the bell was an accomplishment that had seemed unachievable for so many days and nights. I chose to embrace this moment and worry about the future later. In the meantime, I had a new life to live.

Hayes reaches across me to ring the golden bell.

17

NEW BEGINNINGS

*W*ith the bell ceremony in the rearview mirror, our new life could begin. Our family was learning what it was like to be together again. We hadn't spent more than a few consecutive weeks together since early January.

It's amazing how exhausting this phase was. Adrenaline had been carrying us through treatment. We had been so focused on the next step that we almost didn't have time to feel tired. But this summer, we were exhausted. It was similar to the way I felt following a football game. I never felt tired or worn out during the game—it was usually four hours later when the muscles would ache or my head would hurt from the blows I had taken and given.

Our bond as a family was growing. The summer nights were filled with activities, and the kids were busy getting ready for the start a new school year. We had a giant block party one evening, and we released green balloons into the air as a celebration of Hayes. Our kids needed that block party to celebrate the giant milestone. We had bounce houses, kissing booths, and food trucks. Hundreds of people showed up, many we had never met before. We spent that evening with the army that had stood behind the past seven months, thanking each of them for their love and support.

Aside from this block party, one thing that was apparent that summer was that our kids didn't need huge celebrations or big events for entertaining. All they craved was normalcy. So simple things, like watching a movie together or summer walks around the neighborhood, were all they wanted. We had an entire list of things we wanted to do as a family that included late-night baseball games, fireworks, hikes, marshmallow roasting, and movie nights.

Hayes was still our focus, in fact, he was our entertainment. We would celebrate each milestone that he reached physically. The chemotherapy had taken such a toll on his little body that he was still unable to crawl or even roll over. Despite the continuous physical therapy appointments, his body hadn't rebounded. It was understandable for him to be lagging developmentally given the toxicity of the chemotherapy.

But what Hayes lacked physically, he made up for mentally. His desire was there and the fight was alive inside him. There was one moment when we laid Hayes on his stomach to encourage him to roll over. The entire family was gathered around the living room cheering him on as he wiggled his frail hips back and forth. His mind was working, and the determination was kicking in—despite hating being on his stomach. He wiggled his little body to the left, and then to his right, before quickly picking up the pace back and forth, finally rolling over.

"Yeah!" we all said with sheer excitement in our voices. He looked at us with his giant eyes swelling with pride, and moved his legs up and down with bliss. We could sense he felt accomplished for doing something that pleased us. After all, that's what brought joy to Hayes. Hearing us cheer in approval was a big motivator.

For Savanna and I, those summer days were filled with our regular routines like putting the babies to bed and hanging out with the older kids. We would catch up on our reality television shows after the older kids had gone to bed. Many nights, while catching up on these mind-numbing shows, we would sneak upstairs to check on the babies, as we used to do when they were infants. We would often take Hayes out of his crib and bring him downstairs with us, just to cuddle. There was no reason other than just getting some alone time with him at home. He was getting the special treatment, because he was special. He would lay there with us and just hang out, smiling and cuddling on our chests. We wallowed in the independence, without hospital chords attached or monitors to worry about. He was free for us to enjoy just as it should be. Our baby boy was home with us, under one roof with our other five kids. Those moments were simple, but they were so cherished.

The Tate family poses at the photo booth during their summer block party.

I never wanted to leave his side. To be honest, I became kind of needy. Remember when I told you I am a bit of a girl? Yeah, especially when it came to spending time with Hayes. I craved being around him and often found myself dreading going to the office. I even hated things like mowing the lawn because it meant that

I would be away from Hayes. So one day, I got the idea to take Hayes with me by strapping him to my back with one of our hiking backpacks. He rested on my back, with his pacifier in his mouth and a grin surrounding it, as I made my way around the yard. He was happy to be out of the house with me. Once again, it was something extremely simple, and was symbolic of our new life together. We could make memories from even the tedious things, like mowing the lawn. These were things that would've never been the stuff of memories before, but after what we had been through, I didn't pass on any opportunity to be with him.

We were adjusting nicely to this new life and, in some ways, slowly forgetting that Hayes was still battling this awful disease. Except for the fact that he was still on so many different medications. When Savanna wasn't chasing kids around the house or making dinner, she was giving Hayes his medicines or flushing his central line by injecting saline and heparin. Our house was a mini pharmacy.

Another way in which we were moving forward was contributing to awareness of childhood cancer and the lack of funding for research. It's a total disgrace that less than 4 percent of the money raised for cancer research actually goes toward finding treatments and a cure. We felt we were not only a voice for Hayes, we also had a big enough footprint in the childhood cancer world that we could be a voice for other children who suffered similarly.

I reached out to the University of Utah athletic department to start a campaign that would highlight kids around the state who are facing cancer. They were incredibly supportive of the idea, and selected a big football game to feature Hayes on the jumbotron. When the University of Utah played the Washington Huskies, a game featuring two top-ranked teams, media outlets from all over the country would come into Salt Lake City. It turned out to be an extremely competitive battle, yet when our video appeared in the third quarter, the entire audience sat in silence—all eyes turned to the massive television screen. I told our story in a one-minute video to 47,000 people. You could've heard a pin drop in that stadium.

It was an incredibly special moment for our family, but more importantly, it brought awareness to the greater, overlooked issue. Our kids deserve more than 4 percent, and Savanna and I were determined to be a voice for them as well as Hayes.

The next few months were full of football. A washed-up, has-been, collegiate football player has to get his kicks in somehow, so I coach Bo's ten-year-old football team. Hayes offered a common motivational theme during practices and games. I would often talk about how football isn't about how big you are or how fast you are, football is about competing and not backing down despite the odds against you. Football is about being tough—and toughness didn't require being big, fast, or even athletic. It was a mentality. Hayes demonstrated that mentality by fighting a grown-up disease much better than any grown-up could fight it. The kids bought into that the entire season. We played for Hayes that year.

Savanna would bring him to every game and even to some of the practices. The other babies weren't as lucky, but Hayes was special, remember? He could do anything he wanted.

The season was changing into autumn, and the babies continued to provide much of the entertainment for our family. One day, Savanna and I got a random idea to dress them up in costumes. Halloween had nothing to do with it, our motivation was pure fun. So every Sunday we dressed the babies up in a new costume and posted photos on Instagram. It was a big hit. I mean, who doesn't love babies dressed up as adults or characters from their favorite 80s movie? Our initial intent was to get laughs from our followers, but it became something our entire family looked forward to. To be honest, I was all in for about two weeks, but then resented the tradition. Savanna loved it, but she was the one taking the pictures while I was doing all kinds of juggling acts to get the babies to stop crying or to look at the camera. I spent many Sunday afternoons sweating profusely just to get a few online laughs. Still, it was truly therapeutic to shed many tears of laughter each time we dressed them up in a ridiculous costume.

They included many classic movies, including *Back to the Future* with Hayes dressed up as Doc. We dressed them up as old people and circus performers. *Ferris Bueller's Day Off* was also a theme one week, and Hayes made a great Ferris. *The Sandlot, Sound of Music, Indiana Jones*, and *The Hangover* were all featured. While our initial intent was our own mirth, the photo releases soon became an event that everyone looked forward to, including *Huffington Post Canada*. They featured the triplets and our family.

In some ways, these baby dress-up moments were symbolic of how we approached the entire year. We were finding light after darkness. This light also evoked life before cancer struck, when we found a pure joy in raising three little human beings.

In preparation for the upcoming Christmas card season, Savanna and I both felt the need to get family portraits done before the weather got too bad. So on a beautiful fall evening, we made our way up the mountain just fifteen minutes from our home. It was cold and breezy, with a sky was full of clouds, and a slight wind coming from the east. From a photography standpoint, the lighting was ideal. Savanna had coordinated outfits for the entire family and everyone matched each other really well.

As we began taking pictures, a stream of light broke through the clouds and shined onto our family. It was extremely peaceful and warming. There was one moment, which the photographer captured, when we were all hiking up the mountain. I am holding Hayes in one arm, and Wes's hand in the other. Wes is also holding hands with Savanna as she holds Heath. Bo and Mia are following us with little Reese holding onto Bo's head from a perch on his shoulders. It is my favorite picture taken that day, because I feel it captures our family of eight perfectly and is extremely symbolic of the year we had just experienced.

The reason for this is Hayes. In the photo, his cute little body is turned away from the camera to look back at the rest of his family. Hayes is leading us in this picture, peering back at the rest of his family as if to say, "Follow me." We had all been following Hayes throughout this journey as he taught us to press forward during difficult times. The picture captures exactly what we had been through in this fight.

Hayes had been teaching us how to live. It turns out that life is not about enduring challenges, it's about living well despite having challenges. Some people on the outside may judge us for being too confident or hopeful, or perhaps for finding laughter in times of crisis. Everyone has their way of coping with life's challenges, and there isn't a right or wrong way of doing it. We chose to live life rather than endure life. There is a saying I heard growing up: "Endure to the end." How miserable does that sound? The definition of the word *endure* means "to suffer patiently." If that's what life is about, then don't sign me up. Go ahead and pull the cord from me now. I'll just "live to the end." Because that's what Hayes was teaching me to do.

The babies pose as characters from *The Sandlot*.

18

DISNEYLAND

I had promised the kids a trip to Disneyland when Hayes got better. It had been my way of trying to make good of the difficulties they too would face during his treatment. They needed something to look forward to when things got hard, and I guess it worked. We got through it together and were thriving as a family.

November arrived, and so did the Tate Disneyland adventure. As we were packing for the trip, I reflected back to when we found out we were having triplets, and an ad on my phone for Disneyland had induced a panic attack. Between paying for it and the pure chaos of dragging—okay, more like chasing—six kids around the theme park, a glimpse of a giant mouse hadn't seemed worth it.

Now, I happen to love Disneyland, in a healthy way—without that extreme crap you see. I wasn't about to get a Donald Duck tattoo on my lower back any time soon. After all, you should realize by now that I'm more of a Pluto kind of guy. Growing up, I had really enjoyed Disneyland. My dad always made vacations there special for our family. He would buy each of us a souvenir, and I picked the classic Mickey Mouse hat with ears that popped up. I wore it proudly all around the park. I wanted my kids to experience that kind of fun.

So packing my bags for something so important to me, which I once considered impossible, was mind blowing.

"We are really doing this!" I said to Savanna. She didn't respond because, well, Savanna's not a big fan of Disneyland. I know, I agree, there must be something seriously messed up in her brain for not liking the "happiest place on earth." The poor thing never went to Disneyland until I took her after we had been married a few years. So she had no childhood memories that might propel her to take her own children.

We loaded up the car and made our way to Newport Beach, California. You're probably wondering what the hell we were thinking driving to California. Don't worry, it's only a ten-hour drive, no big deal. That's a breeze with three screaming babies and three older kids who want to pull each other's hair out. Amazingly, it was one of the funniest drives of our lives, despite some moments of tears and sibling wrestling matches. The older kids took up the third row of the suburban with electronics to keep them happy, while the babies in the second row watched *Baby Einstein* on two iPads.

Savanna and I talked the entire way. It is incredible how we can spend five hours straight in conversation and never run out of things to say. Most couples get to that boring point in the relationship when they no longer have anything to say to each other. But Savanna and I could spend days talking nonstop, some of which is gossip, but don't judge us. We never left the honeymoon stage of our marriage. We have been married for twelve years and every day is full of entertainment and love.

Of course we felt a need to document our trip. We were rolling the GoPro camera a lot during the car ride, even during our frequent stops. First off, it seemed like Wes had a bladder the size of an almond. And we stopped just to take pictures of the family at various sites, especially in front of the beautiful red rocks of Southern Utah. We cruised the Strip in Las Vegas and walked around on a sunny morning. Judging by the stares and head turns, we could get our own show at a casino. We were a freak show of eight, but we were owning it as a special time together.

Even the road trip carried much less stress and worry than in the past, and those trips never involved three babies. Reese and Heath could tantrum all they liked, I was cool. Hayes was behind me in his car seat, enjoying every moment.

"What's Hayes doing?" I would ask Savanna. She would peer back and see him looking out the window with the usual calmness on his face.

We finally arrived at the Newport Beach hotel and got inside. The kids were so excited to see the room. It was big and overlooked the ocean.

"This is amazing! Thanks Dad," they said as they made their way from room to room. Even the babies felt it was magical being in a new place with different furniture they could now ruin.

"How amazing is this?" Savanna asked rhetorically. "I'm so glad we're doing this," she said, grabbing the inside of my bicep and squeezing. She held her head on my shoulder as we watched all six of our kids running and jumping around the hotel room.

There were a lot of items that we had on our agenda for this trip and one of those included relaxing at the beach. The next morning, we headed to Balboa island to visit the pier and get some time in the sand. It was 85 degrees, with not a person in sight. I have never seen a beach so quiet and calm in all my years of visiting California. We had the entire beach to ourselves and we made the most of it. The kids ran up and down the pier with Reese and Heath, now almost twenty-months old, following like little ducklings. I held Hayes and enjoyed the warmth of the sun beating down.

We made our way to the beach, and the kids wasted no time getting into the waves. There was a playground close by, a perfect place to entertain the babies. Savanna took Reese and Heath to the slide and I carried Hayes to the swing set. I remember walking toward it with an overwhelming sense of gratitude. I picked Hayes up and placed him in the black seat that seemed custom fit for his little frog legs. Hesitant at first, he settled in. Then he stared up at me with his baby-blue eyes.

Hayes's eyes have always been special, but in this particular moment there was very little doubt they were speaking directly to my soul. His eyes were telling a story. I stared back at him, fixated, and was overcome with emotion: it felt as though he was thanking me. Thanking me for taking him to this special place without physicians or nurses. His eyes were also thanking me for the previous year, during which I never left his side. I failed to hold back tears. Our souls connected more strongly than ever before. My body was numb, oblivious to anything and everything around me. I felt warmth throughout my body as I began swinging him back and forth. I was focused on his eyes, and his on mine. There was a smile on his face as he enjoyed the back and forth movement. The sun was reflecting off his dirty blonde hair.

Wiping tears from my face, I couldn't help but think to myself how perfect the moment was. Hayes's once-bald head was filled with beautiful, thick, blonde hair. There were no tubes to hold him back from the sway of the swing. The sun was shining down on his angelic little body, a sun that had once been shielded by hospital walls. His feet were dangling as if relieved and feeling a sense of independence. *Hayes is a little boy today,* I thought, *not a child sick with a life-threatening disease.* The days and nights stuck in a hospital room were a distant memory. Hayes was finally experiencing freedom. He was experiencing boyhood and life, and so was I.

Hayes swinging at a playground on Balboa Beach.

The older kids could be overheard laughing and screaming in joy as they were chased by waves. I briefly turned to watch the three of them enjoying themselves. They were no longer fearing for their little brother, and his cancer was no longer hanging over them. They had each other and everything they needed at that moment.

This moment was Heavenly. I know that sounds a bit cliché, but it was truly straight from Heaven. I felt a presence surround me and Hayes, one that was unparalleled to any other moment in my life.

The next morning was a beautiful Tuesday. We had purchased a two-day pass at Disneyland, and this was the first day. We got the kids ready for the much-anticipated trip. Their excitement was palpable.

"I can't wait to go on the Indiana Jones ride," Bo said while he did his hair. Wes and Mia were excited to see the Disneyland characters in person.

"I want to meet Anna," Mia said to Wes as they argued back and forth about which Disney character we were going to meet first.

Savanna had bought the kids Disney-themed T-shirts to wear. The babies were decked out in Mickey Mouse shirts with their names underneath the mouse ears. We arrived and as we walked inside, the kids' eyes grew wide.

"Mom, look! It's Mickey!" Wes said, pointing to his left. The older three kids picked up the pace and started running toward the giant mouse. Savanna was holding Hayes, and I was pushing Heath and Reese in the stroller trying to keep up. The line was relatively short and then it was their turn to meet Mickey Mouse. Savanna had Hayes in her arms, and his eyes were fixated on the character. One of Hayes's favorite shows was *Mickey Mouse Clubhouse*. He would watch it every morning, both in the hospital and at home. His smile would widen, be followed by a few giggles, and he often clapped when he heard the theme song.

Savanna moved to get the perfect picture of the older kids next to Mickey. She tried to maneuver Hayes's body just right, but she was having some difficulty positioning him in a way that would allow her to snap a photo.

Hayes looks up at Mickey during the family trip to Disneyland.

"This is Hayes," she said to Mickey. "He just got done with seven months of chemotherapy. He's our little cancer fighter." Mickey stopped his usual fidgeting and waving. He knelt down, shifted his weight, and sat cross-legged, indicating that Savanna should place Hayes in his lap.

Hayes's reaction was priceless. He couldn't stop looking up at Mickey's face. At one point, he reached up and grabbed Mickey's nose. It was as if he knew the importance of this magical moment. People often describe Disneyland as magical, and we were seeing magic happen before our eyes. This brief interaction between Hayes and Mickey was extraordinary. Hayes was trying to look into the mouse's eyes, as he does with anyone and everyone he comes into contact with. He was trying to tell Mickey his story, and I got the sense that Mickey understood how special the moment was. Obviously, Mickey meets a lot of children each day, but I sensed that he felt Hayes's spirit glowing through his crystal blue eyes. His attention was no longer distracted by the people walking by or those in line. He was embracing this moment with our special little boy.

Bo holds Hayes in his arms as he looks up at Mickey Mouse.

There was no way of topping that moment, but we didn't need to. Whatever happened next was irrelevant. This is what we had come for, and Hayes's moment with Mickey was worth the price of admission—which is saying a lot when it's coming from me, the tightwad.

We did the usual Disneyland things after that, which entailed waiting in longs lines and walking through crowds. I'm not going to lie, it was the most exhausting afternoon of my entire life. I had done some intense workouts in my life, but nothing topped a day at Disneyland. We had packed lunches for the kids and snacks for the babies that were meant to last the entire day and through the evening. Yeah, well, that didn't happen. I ate everything in that bag by 11 a.m. I ate soggy peanut butter sandwiches, fish crackers, and Oreos. I didn't even hold back from eating the apple sauce in a little, squeezable pouch. I felt as though I was lugging around a bunch of bowling balls in my arms, except these bowling balls were little ninjas who fought to escape my arms every time we waited in a line.

I remember waiting in line for the Dumbo ride with two babies in my arms while Savanna was holding another. My back was sopping wet with sweat. If the meeting with Hayes and Mickey was Heaven, this was definitely hell. But then I realized that wasn't an accurate assessment. Hell isn't hanging out at Disneyland with over-anxious kids. Hell is being in a hospital room while chemotherapy is being administered to your son. That reminder was a good wakeup call that allowed me to relax and roll with the moments of stress to enjoy the rest of the day at Disneyland.

We did enjoy it. The kids were happy. I loved watching the joy in their faces as they walked around. We took the entire family on Pirates of the Caribbean and laughed when the babies got scared. That sounds a little mean, but there is something abnormally cute when a baby gets scared. We all giggled as they would turn to hide their faces in our shoulders. We made so many memories that day.

We needed the next day to recover, so we spent it at the hotel pool. The kids were enjoying each other's company, which was a miracle in itself. Our oldest Bo tends to pick on Mia, Mia then picks on Wes, and Wes passes it down to Heath. Reese and Hayes seem to get a pass. The weather was unusually perfect for mid-November. I spent the day teaching Wes how to swim while the other kids ran back and forth from the hot tub to the pool. The babies were still worn out and spent most the afternoon napping inside the hotel room. Even the moments of downtime were enjoyable. We spent our nights hanging out and renting movies. Savanna and I were even able to enjoy late-night talks in the hot tub while Bo watched over things. We were all gaining energy and love by being together.

The next day, we headed for one more day of Disneyland fun. It wasn't as eventful, but in some ways that was just fine. We watched a Christmas parade that included some of the kids' favorite characters. Hayes was mesmerized watching the floats go up and down Main Street. I soaked up every opportunity to observe each of my kids once again.

The day of activities was coming to an end. We had crossed off all the things the kids had planned to do, from Thunder Mountain to It's a Small World. We made one last stop at Cars Land. Savanna hopped in line with one of the kids to go on a last ride before we made our way out of the park. I stayed back with the other kids, including the babies. Christmas music was playing throughout Disneyland, and caught in the spirit, I picked up Hayes and held him as I swayed back and forth to "White Christmas."

As I danced with him, I thought back to the previous Christmas when Hayes's symptoms had begun to show. I recalled how his frail little body would fight just to lift his head. I thought about the moment he was diagnosed, and that scary afternoon when we saw the horrific CT scan. This gave me more reason to hold Hayes a little tighter that night, knowing that this second life he was experiencing was a blessing.

It was amazing how fast the week flew by, which is always a sign of a successful trip. With only two more nights left in sunny California, we spent the next two days at the beach and by the pool. We had come across a family friendly playground and spent a few hours each day hanging out in the sand and chasing the kids around the playground.

*****

On November 13, we loaded up the car and made our way back to Utah. It's always a sad feeling heading back home after a week of fun. But this seemed even a little more depressing than usual, probably because we had looked forward to it so incredibly much. So it was harder now that it had already come and gone. It had been a week without worry or fear, without doctors or nurses surrounding us. There were no mind-consuming worries in the kids' eyes. Their innocence had been retrieved this week. They were enjoying this time with their little brother, as they often looked at Hayes to see the happiness he was experiencing. Just as I did.

This trip had been a vacation from cancer, and the drive home felt like leaving paradise and reentering the real world. We were entering a previous world in which cancer existed. Because we had gone an entire week without Hayes throwing up—until that car ride back to Salt Lake City.

19

THE PHONE CALL

The fact that Hayes was throwing up again was not so unusual. He had been throwing up, off and on, since he received the G-tube as a means for nutrition. There is typically a big learning curve when it comes to feeding a child with a G-tube. Sometimes we were overfeeding him, which led to vomiting, and other times we weren't feeding him enough. We had spent the past few months figuring out what worked best for Hayes and his digestive system. In addition, Hayes was developing some reflux from the baby formula.

"We did change formulas for the week in California," Savanna said as she was brainstorming other possible reasons for the increase in frequency.

"That makes sense," I replied. We were all trying to get back into the swing of things. The kids had missed a week of school and had loads of homework to catch up on. The babies were also readjusting to a more typical schedule. We all seemed a little worn out from the vacation, but the memories we made were still fresh in our minds.

A few days went by as we continued to monitor Hayes closely. We got him back on the regular formula and tweaked his feeding routine a few times, in hopes of identifying the reason for the vomiting. His mood was happy, which is typical for Hayes, even during his darkest moments. His energy levels were surprisingly high and his physical appearance was healthy. We were experts at monitoring Hayes, and knew him inside and out, so our level of concern about the vomiting was still relatively low.

Our initial reflux diagnosis faded once we had adjusted him back to his previous diet. The vomiting was not subsiding. "Maybe he got a little stomach bug in California," Savanna said as we were lying in bed one night talking about our little boy once again. It's amazing how fast reality hit us, just a few days removed from our paradisiacal vacation. Four days before, we had been dancing in the streets of Disneyland. And now Savanna and I were lying in bed trying to figure out what was causing Hayes to feel sick. We went through our usual parental checklist, which everyone who has experienced childhood cancer knows all too well. Hayes didn't have the typical fever, so we weren't worried too intensely.

"I don't think it's a bug, babe. None of the other babies are throwing up." I wracked my brain trying to put my finger on what was going on. We were both exhausted that night, still recovering from the vacation. As we were both dozing, I had a distinct thought: *consider the shunt.* It is common for brain cancer patients, particularly those with brain tumors, to need a shunt. It acts as drainage for the brain and allows natural brain fluid to be distributed to the rest of the body. Since Hayes's brain tumor had been excessive, he needed to have a temporary shunt placed to prevent excessive fluid in the brain.

At this point, Savanna was already asleep. Of course she was asleep, she can sleep through a dump truck driving through a nitroglycerine plant. I credit to the best Christmas movie of all time, *National Lampoon's Christmas Vacation*, for that quote. So when we awoke in the morning I immediately told Savanna of the impression to check on Hayes's shunt.

"That would make sense," she responded.

"Maybe there's some pressure in his head or something," I said, trying to think through the impression I received the night before.

"I'll call the physician and take him in," Savanna said, picking up the phone and calling our oncologist.

It was some sort of twilight zone, or déjà vu. We were in the exact same shoes as we were almost a year ago, trying to figure out what was wrong with Hayes. Fortunately, this go-around we didn't waste time with family practice physicians who are ill-equipped to find the cause for his vomiting. We were extremely frustrated that this was being thrown at us immediately after the best vacation of our entire lives. Perhaps it was the sense of freedom we felt while we were in California: eight days without worry or stress about cancer or chemotherapy, a glimpse of what the possible future could be like, and renewed hope that the worst was behind us. As we were now shocked into understanding, it had been a false hope, one that had tricked our mind into thinking Hayes was done with that evil world, home free.

A few hours after the phone call, Savanna and I were on our way to Primary Children's Hospital. We made our way to the fourth floor, which was extremely emotional. It hadn't been that long, just over 100 days, since we had left for what we hoped would be the last time, Now we were walking right back into the nightmare. Our PTSD was kicking us straight in the face, and Savanna and I both had tears in our eyes as we worked our way back to a room. Our hearts were beating and the nerves were kicking in.

I took Hayes into the ER after symptoms got worse.

We sat there waiting for the physician, knowing that this visit wasn't due to a simple stomach bug or reflux. We knew it wasn't a change in diet, though we had certainly hoped for those things. While we were praying our hearts out for a diagnosis like those, our instincts were letting us know it was much more than that.

"Hayes!" the oncologist said as she opened the opened the door. "It's good to see you with so much hair. He looks so good," she said as she sat down next to us to do her usual examination. She was happy to see Hayes. I wish we could've said the same thing about seeing her. It wasn't as though we didn't like her or appreciate her, but seeing her wasn't something I had on my list of things to do before the new year. There was very little doubt that Hayes had left an impression on her and the staff who had cared for him this past year. Apparently there was still a picture of our sweet little boy hanging in their break room.

"What's been going on with our little Hayes?" she asked, looking at Savanna for an explanation.

"He started throwing up on the last day of our trip, which was five days ago," Savanna answered. I was standing up with my back leaning against the wall. I was extremely anxious being in that hospital room. I couldn't shake the impression I had received the night before. If it was his shunt, it would require an additional surgery. I was extremely apprehensive about putting Hayes through another surgery, not because I didn't think he could handle it, but rather I cringed at the thought of another scar on his head. Hayes's head had five scars on it. That's right, five previous surgeries.

"Do you think this could be related to this shunt?" I interrupted as the physician was looking into Hayes's eyes with a light.

"That's certainly a possibility," she said as she moved an object from side to side and vertically. Hayes followed it with his eyes. "From a cognitive functionality standpoint, he appears to be healthy. He is focusing really well and seems to be engaged during the tests I performed," she said, and my nerves rested momentarily.

"Obviously, my initial concern is a possible return of the brain tumor. Based on the tests I just performed, there doesn't appear to be a mass buildup in his brain," she said.

I was caught off guard. I never even thought about the possibility of a mass in his brain.

"Let's go ahead and get a CT scan for better analysis," she said, and she texted the radiology department to give them a heads up.

The CT scan took fifteen minutes. The results would come much quicker than an MRI, but also lack the in-depth images. Savanna was entertaining Hayes with some videos on Youtube while we waited. PTSD was in high gear as our nerves were building in anticipation. It's amazing how quickly your perspective changes. Initially, I had been dreading an additional surgery, but suddenly that became best-case scenario. Surgery is an easy solution compared to the alternative. I couldn't come close fathoming more chemotherapy treatments.

"Well, your initial thought was accurate," the doctor said as she walked in the room. "Some additional fluid has built up in his brain. This is the reason for his increased vomiting. Based on its location, we will need to put in an additional shunt to free the fluid." Our discouragement must have been evident. It was a week before Thanksgiving and we had envisioned a holiday with all six healthy kids. I mean, we knew Hayes wasn't exactly "healthy", but all we wanted was a normal, boring Thanksgiving.

The doctor continued. "We can actually do the surgery first thing in the morning tomorrow. Then you would be home with your family for Thanksgiving." She was trying to ease our minds, and it certainly helped. After a few phone calls to the neurosurgeons, we were admitted to the hospital fifteen minutes later and scheduled for surgery in the morning.

Hayes was familiar with the hospital rooms, almost too comfortable. He knew the routine. He had all the television shows he wanted and knew the staff. It was his home away from home. Sadly, he actually knew hospital rooms better than his room at our house. When the neurosurgeon came in the discuss the surgery, he said he needed an MRI first. That would give him more precision during the procedure. Just hearing "MRI" gave me extreme anxiety. Regardless of the reason for this MRI, I dreaded what would follow because I knew oncology would want to use it to review the current state of the cancer. I didn't want to receive any bad news, especially before the upcoming Christmas season. I wanted to spend Christmas as an entire family, with Hayes at home.

Hayes sleeping in his hospital crib.

Savanna stayed the night with Hayes while I went home. It was a Friday night. I remember when Friday nights used to be exciting, during our pre-cancer life. Savanna and I would try to go on dates. We loved grabbing some dinner and going to movies together, but those days were now long gone. We didn't even get to sleep under the same roof.

We weren't as nervous with this MRI because results came in on a Saturday, which meant the oncology team wouldn't review them until Monday. We had some time before facing the hardest stuff. The procedure came and went, and seemed to be successful. The neurosurgeon informed Savanna and I that everything went as planned. "We will hold him here overnight and see how he's doing in the morning before we agree to release him. I don't anticipate that he'll be here for more than two days, but we'll see how he does."

We were hopeful that this procedure would alleviate the pressure Hayes was feeling in his head. The doctors certainly believed that the fluid had been causing the vomiting, so we felt confident that he would soon feel much better with it gone.

But Hayes got really sick, and threw up all night. Savanna was concerned. "It's frustrating," she said to me over the phone, fighting back the tears, "he's so miserable." She spoke softly, in a depleted way. My heart immediately sunk into my stomach. Savanna was worried, which takes quite a bit, so I felt extremely concerned. She doesn't get flustered easily, but there was fear in her voice that day.

The doctors came to evaluate Hayes a few hours later. They were actually pleased with the way he was acting, with little concern about the vomiting. Apparently it takes time to adjust to changes in pressure. They were confident that it would subside over the next few days and that he would start feeling better. Savanna and I were extremely relieved; after all, physicians were the ones with experience, they had seen this thousands of times. Hours later, we were released from the hospital.

We were really excited to have Hayes home, especially because we were only a few days away from Thanksgiving. But we were hesitant to feel hopeful or stress-free until we saw signs of the old Hayes. Because even at home, Hayes was nauseous and continued to throw up every few hours. Each time he did, we became more and more paranoid. The words of the physician replayed in my brain, over and over again: the pressure change would make Hayes feel nauseous. Each time I felt my anxiety level go sky high, I would remind myself of those words.

On Monday I went to the office. I would check in with Savanna every hour or so to see how our little boy was doing. Being at the office served as a distraction from worry, in some way, but I was basically unproductive. I couldn't focus on anything other than Hayes. She sent me a few pictures of Hayes and informed me that he appeared to feel better. One of the pictures was of Hayes with Reese and Heath. All three of them seemed content in the picture, which made me smile. Hayes was with his siblings and they were enjoying themselves—as they should be. He deserved that moment and many more like it.

I watched the clock all day before, finally, it was time to head home. I opened the door to the house and was greeted by our little Reese. She must've sensed I was coming home and waited for me to swing open the door. I picked her up and gave her a giant kiss on the cheek. Reese had developed a little neediness for me since Savanna had spent the past year at the hospital. She had turned into a Daddy's girl.

I walked into the kitchen and saw Savanna making dinner. Mia was seated at the dining room table doing homework and Heath was wandering around the house. I walked over to Savanna, hugged her, and asked about her day. Hayes was sitting in his favorite rocker chair. I walked over, picked him up, and tossed him slightly in the air to get him to smile. He smiled, of course, despite not feeling well. I set him back down, and then Savanna's phone rang. She answered in a shaky, hesitant voice, which led me to believe it was a doctor and it was serious.

"What? Oh no!" she said, gasping for air. Her hand covered her eyes in disbelief. I couldn't hear the conversation, but I didn't need to. I understood everything from Savanna's reaction. Tears began flowing from her face and she fell to the floor, still gripping the phone to her ear. I knelt to wipe the tears from her cheek. She was not talking, only listening and gasping for air.

Mia was only a few feet from us. "Dad, what's wrong?" she asked, standing to see her mom on the floor in tears. She watched as Savanna curled into the fetal position, barely able to breath.

"Hey Mia, could you go get Reese and take her into the playroom?" I replied to find some way of distracting her. I felt so torn at this moment: should I comfort Savanna or the eight year old who just witnessed her mom fall to the floor, shaking? While my wife lay there, receiving the worst news of her life, I stood and gave Mia a hug. Her sweet little face was in shock and filled with concern. After a little encouragement, she left the room with Reese.

Savanna's entire body was shaking, back and forth, with each breath she took. Her breaths were light and quick, panicked. The coloring in her face was gone and she kicked the ground in anger and fear. She held the phone in one hand and covered her face with the other. I felt helpless. Seated beside her, I hugged her as she sobbed.

My mind was racing to imagine what was being said on the other end. All I knew was that it was devastating news. My eyes filled with tears as I tried to remain calm and strong for my wife. That conversation seemed to last an hour, but wasn't more than five minutes. The longest five minutes of our lives.

IT'S BACK

When the conversation ended, Savanna dropped the phone on the hardwood floor. She was still in the fetal position, with me leaning over her in an attempt to provide some warmth and comfort. Mia had returned to the kitchen with Reese in her arms. We laid there for a few minutes before I encouraged Savanna to get up and head to our bedroom. I was extremely curious about the conversation, but I dreaded hearing the details at the same time. As I helped Savanna up the stairs, in hopes of finding some privacy to discuss the call, her body was almost crippled with sorrow.

We sat on the bed and I was extremely hesitant, but asked, "What did she say?" I already knew that it had been our oncologist. Savanna was still trying to catch her breath, she had such a shock to her system. Her hands were shaking uncontrollably as she covered her face with them. All I could do was hug her.

In the past year, I had come to know that it's almost harder to relay devastating news than it is to hear it. Your mind goes into shock and there are moments of complete denial. It's as if your new reality might stay untrue, that is, until the moment you say the words.

"It's back," she managed to say at last.

"It's back? Oh no!" I said as I put my head in my hands. "What did she say is the next step?" My question was asked in typical husband fashion. One of the duties as a husband and dad is to fix things.

During Hayes's diagnosis and treatments, that was the hardest things for me to relinquish. I wanted to fix his cancer. I wanted to take the pain away from Hayes. I wanted to take the sadness away from my kids and Savanna. This is what dads are supposed to do, right?

"It...has...spread," she was pausing in between each word to breathe. "To his...brainstem."

Saying the words must have been excruciating. During the early days of the diagnosis, Savanna's worst fear was relapse. I was more concerned about the treatments working, and she had reassured me that the treatments were going to work—it was relapse that we needed to worry about. Her nightmare had just become reality.

"What are our options?" I asked, once again searching for the solution rather than digesting the fact that his cancer was back, in the worst location in the brain. I had done enough research to understand the limitations of additional therapy for Hayes's type of cancer. We had already taken the most aggressive approach with the Head Start II protocol. So even as I asked, I knew options were extremely limited.

"She said," Savanna began before her voice faltered. "She said, 'You can try at-home chemotherapy, radiation, or...'" she trailed off, not wanting to finish the sentence. "Or, they can just make him comfortable." She let out a loud gasp.

"Make him comfortable?" I asked, aghast. I didn't need elaboration. I knew what that meant. It meant the cancer was aggressive. It meant there was very little hope. I knew this, and it started to sink in.

I began crying and my hands went numb. My lips began to tingle. I was going into shock as I laid my head down on the pillow. At first, I covered my face in hopes of somehow hiding it from Savanna. I was trying to be strong for her, but as the reality sunk in, there was no hiding. I sobbed from the fear of losing Hayes.

"I don't want to lose him!" I said, with desperation in my voice.

We both lay on the bed crying. No additional words were needed, we were both just trying to comprehend it. *How could it happen so fast?* I thought. *Just ten days ago I was at the beach with Hayes, experiencing the greatest joy in my life, and now this. How is that even possible?*

I had always known his cancer was extremely aggressive. He had been only nine months old at diagnosis, and the tumor was the size of a large lemon, so it didn't take a medical degree to understand the severity of this cancer. Regardless, trying to comprehend the severity once it had returned felt impossible.

It made sense that Savanna had felt he was getting better, because that's typical. That was how it happened when he was first diagnosed: the symptoms tended to come and go. There were moments when we felt he had turned the corner toward health, and then the pressure would mount in his little brain until the only way to get relief was through vomiting.

There were no words that would make any of it better, but I felt a need to break the silence and provide some sort of strength. "We are going to get through this," I said, combing through Savanna's hair with my hand. I didn't know how we would get through it, but I knew we had a love that was deep and unbreakable. We had already been through the trenches of hell as a couple, so I never for an instant feared an inability to manage pain or dark times.

After about a half hour, we slowly picked ourselves up and crawled out of bed. It was somewhat symbolic of what he had done the entire year. We had been knocked down before, but we weren't about to let it keep us down too long. We were going to fight with every fiber of our being until the very end. Savanna slowly got up enough energy to hold her body upright and wrapped her arms around me.

"I don't wanna lose you," she said as she pressed her head against my chest.

It took me off guard. "What do you mean?"

It's always been in Savanna's nature to worry about me, often times before she worried about herself. She knew the bond I had with Hayes, and perhaps feared for my mental health. Perhaps she feared for our marriage if Hayes lost this battle.

I reassured her of my love. "Babe, we are going to get through this together. You don't need to worry about me," I said as I grabbed her face and looked directly into her eyes.

We then made our way downstairs to talk to the kids. I had already had some difficult conversations with them, but this one was excruciating to face. It would be even more difficult to explain things to the kids than it had been to receive the news. I hated seeing pain in their eyes.

I called for Mia and Wes, and they followed me into the office. Bo was still at basketball practice, so I planned on going over there after I talked to his siblings.

"As you know, we just got a call from Hayes's doctor," I said as I closed the door behind us. Savanna was sitting in my office chair. I got down on one knee to make direct eye contact with their little bodies. "You know how much Mom and Dad love you, right?" I felt like I needed to let them feel love from their dad before I continued. "We love you so much and we love Hayes so much," I reiterated and paused to take a deep breath.

"We have just been told that Hayes's cancer is back." I fought like hell to hold back the tears as the reality sunk in further. Mia immediately broke into tears. Her cute, little, round face turned the color of her reddish hair as she wept. "I am so sorry guys. I would take this away from you. I would take this away from Hayes if I could," I said as tears began falling from my cheeks.

Telling them was one of the harder things I have done as a dad. There's no book or study material that prepares you for moments like that and, if there was, I probably would've read the CliffsNotes version anyway.

"We will continue to fight for Hayes and not give up, just like we would do for each of you," I said confidently. I wanted to make sure they knew I still had hope in my blood. I needed them to know that, although I was sad, it wasn't going to hold me back from getting Hayes the help he needed. Our new fight started that very night.

Since we started this journey, I always made sure that I was the one to relay information to the kids. It was my responsibility as their Dad, as I feared that others wouldn't have the right words. So after talking to Wes and Mia, I left the house quickly to pick Bo up from basketball practice and deliver the news. It was a cold and rainy November night, fitting for what we were experiencing. I pulled into the church parking lot and as I parked the car and tried to build up the courage to walk in, I cried. I wept like I have never wept before. I was alone in my car, which had always been my safe haven, and I let it all out. I yelled in anger and pounded the steering wheel with my fist, asking "Why?" over and over again.

I was so mad. I was angry at cancer and, admittedly, angry at God. I felt like He wasn't listening to my prayers of desperation. I was mad that He didn't prevent this relapse from occurring, and even for the initial diagnosis. I had battled this anger throughout the year, as I often wondered what I had done to deserve this crisis.

I finally settled down enough to grab Bo from his practice. He could sense something was wrong from the redness in my eyes. He knew I had been crying. As we got in the car, I looked at Bo and tried my best to hold back the tears.

"Bo, one of the hardest things I have ever had to do as a dad is to have difficult discussions with you. I hate doing it for you. I hate it for me. But I feel you should hear it from me, because I love you." Once again, I felt the need to express my love for him before continuing: "We just found out that Hayes's cancer is back." I wiped tears from my cheek.

I could see the devastation in his brown eyes. I reached my left arm across my body to embrace him in the passenger seat. I grabbed his head and held it against my chest as he cried. It was a father and son moment, one that I would've much rather avoided, but it is one that we will both never forget. He knew without a doubt that I was there for him. Our love and trust for each other grew in that heartbreaking moment.

Having talked with all the kids, our attention immediately turned to Hayes. The pain was growing and the vomiting and nausea were taking over. We had tried over-the-counter pain medicine, but none of that seemed to relax him or provide comfort. During the dreaded phone call, the oncologist had discussed the need to get Hayes's pain under control. She had encouraged us to check into the hospital if we felt he was uncomfortable or in additional pain. Hayes was extremely tough about pain tolerance, but there were moments that evening when he would scream in discomfort. This pain was much more intense than any of his previous surgeries. We had seen Hayes in some difficult situations, and this was extremely unusual for him. So unusual that we felt he needed to go to the hospital to manage the pain.

We checked into the hospital around 8:30 p.m., and immediately headed to the fourth floor. It was extremely depressing to step into the elevator that night. I had the feeling that this particular visit wasn't going to be a simple overnight stay. Something was telling me that this was much more serious, and that this pain wasn't associated with the shunt surgery.

After three hours or so, Hayes was finally settling down. They had given him some morphine and his body immediately began to relax. Savanna and I were exhausted, but had no desire to sleep that night. I also had no intention of leaving the hospital to be with the kids. I knew that Savanna needed me by her side, and that Hayes needed me. So we made arrangements for my mother-in-law to stay with them, with some additional family members who were in town for Thanksgiving. We spent the entire night tossing and turning on a twin bed next to Hayes's crib.

My thoughts consumed me that night and the raging emotions never ceased. I watched the clock as tears came in waves. The days with my perfect little boy were now limited and I couldn't grasp the idea of life without him. I had feared this day since his diagnosis. This was the nightmare that I had tried to avoid for almost an entire year. When the tumor was removed, I had trained my mind to avoid thinking about life without him, and now I wasn't just thinking about this dark place, I was living it. All the hope that I had built up during treatments was now destroyed. That hope was what had been keeping me sane. There had always been a next step in the treatment, and those next steps gave me hope. They served a larger purpose than just keeping Hayes alive—they were doing the same for me.

Savanna was next to me, awake for most of the night as well. When she did fall asleep, I tried my best not to wake her because although I wanted to talk to her, I wanted her to get some rest. We talked in twenty-minute segments throughout the night, conversations that centered around what we felt would be the best next step for Hayes. The doctor had given us a proposal during the phone call. The next step would be radiation, which they had already scheduled a consultation for the following morning.

Radiation is something Savanna and I had always been strongly against. In fact, we weren't alone in our beliefs about it—our entire team of oncologists were against radiation therapy in children under three years old. It's only used as a last-ditch effort because it is associated with severe cognitive side effects. We had heard hundreds of stories in which radiation had caused children to become severely mentally disabled, even leading to a vegetative state. But we were desperate now. At this point, we were willing to do whatever it took to rid our youngest child from the cancer consuming his brain.

Morning came, the day of the radiation consultation. Savanna and I were still in shock. The hospital room was much quieter than usual. During our previous rounds, we always had fun talking with the staff who we had grown to love. With the amount of time we had spent there, they knew us like family. We got to know them on a very personal level since they offered our only social interactions. But today was different. There were no side conversations in the room, no small talk. In fact, the television hadn't been turned on since we got there. We had no desire to see what was going on outside the hospital, it was completely irrelevant. This was our life and Hayes was the only thing in it at this point. Nothing else mattered.

Hayes was still in a lot of pain. His once beautiful, hopeful eyes were worn out, and his little body was losing weight. He had lost almost two pounds since we checked into the hospital for shunt surgery on Friday afternoon. This equated to losing 10 percent of his bodyweight in less than four days.

The radiation consultation was at the neighboring hospital for adults, which made sense, since radiation wasn't advised in children Hayes's age. We were escorted by security staff to The Huntsman Cancer Institute, one of the premier locations for cancer research and treatment. It was awkward checking into the clinic that day with a room full of adults. It wasn't full of just adults, most of these people were in their latter years. That's a nice way of saying they were old. The waiting room was full of people fighting cancer who had already lived long and prosperous lives. It wasn't right that our little twenty-month-old baby was fighting the same life-threatening illness as this room full of old people. It made me depressed. Every person in that waiting room was dying, in some way or another. They were all in a need of a miracle to come out on top and win against cancer. But I felt as though Hayes deserved the miracle the most. I know that's insensitive, and I felt insensitive for thinking it that day, but I would've given anything in the world for Hayes to experience a long life like theirs. They had witnessed the highs and lows of actual living. Just the simple fact that they had learned to walk made me bitter. My boy hadn't lived long enough to walk yet. It was unfair.

A few minutes later, we were called back to a room where the physician and our regular oncologist were waiting. "Have a seat," the new doctor said as the nurse closed the door behind us.

"As you know, we want to give you additional information on radiation," he said as he sat back in the chair with his arms folded. I immediately got the sense that he was extremely knowledgeable and skilled, and I could also tell from the tone of his voice that he was focused on helping Hayes. He educated us on the possible side effects on a child under three. "There have been cognitive side effects, some severe, as we monitor these children throughout their lives. Many of these side effects only show up years after therapy, sometimes not for six years." He paused momentarily. "For someone like Hayes, based on his current condition...it would be a miracle for him to survive long enough to see any of these side effects."

My hands covered my eyes, and then I pulled my baseball cap over them. It was my attempt to digest the news. The doctor went on. "Based on the severity of his disease, there is no way to prevent this cancer from coming back. Although we have never performed this type of treatment on the cancer Hayes has, I would like to think that we could possibly prolong his life." His tone was hopeful, but nothing he said after that mattered to me. I had been told that my son's condition was terminal.

Me holding Hayes just before the visit with the radiation oncologist.

We had thought this extreme measure might cure him, so we had been considering it as one last-ditch effort to fight his illness entirely, once and for all. Not simply to prolong his life. We had just been told that he wouldn't survive past the age of five. Our hopes of seeing Hayes grow up, go to school, and get married were now over. Those possible memories were no more.

As the doctor told us more about radiation treatment and the timeframe involved, I looked at Hayes as he sat there doped up on morphine. He needed help, or relief, immediately.

"First and foremost," I said sternly, "I want to see Hayes healthy enough to proceed with this treatment, if we choose to go this direction. Right now, he can't even be off the morphine without throwing up."

"We agree with you," the oncologist said, "we will not move forward until Hayes can withstand the treatments and short-term side effects." Cognitive impairments were the long-term side effects, while the short-term side effects were familiar to us from chemotherapy: additional hair loss, vomiting, skin rashes and burns, and fevers associated with low white blood cell counts.

"We will need some time to discuss this with each other," I replied.

"Take your time," she said. "I'll be in the hospital this evening and tomorrow if, and when, you feel like you have decided."

We spent the afternoon talking about the meeting. Our focus was on relieving the pain Hayes was experiencing. We wanted him to have a decent quality of life and having him on a constant morphine drip, as the only way to calm his little body, disturbed both of us.

"I just want him to be comfortable," I said to Savanna, with a note of desperation.

"I agree," she said. "It's hard to even think about the next step in treatment when he's like this. But I will do whatever it takes to keep him alive at this point," her voice began to shake, "even it's only for an additional month."

"Me too," I replied, wrapping my arms around her in that silent hospital room. We both understood the pros and cons of radiation. We understood the slim miracle it would take for Hayes to even reach five years old, and then he may face the long-term side effects.

Suddenly, images of Hayes running around with his triplet brother and sister entered my mind. I would've done anything to see him walk. That was such a giant milestone for me because walking represented freedom and independence. I yearned for Hayes to experience that. I so desperately wanted him to walk around the house with his little frog legs that images of it continued to flood my mind as I talked with Savanna. I also had visions of future birthday celebrations with all three babies. I pictured them as crazy five-year-olds, wrestling in the backyard, throwing baseballs, and swinging a bat.

I'd give anything for that, I thought. Those images never reached beyond five years of age, because after that I saw much uglier images. I saw a boy suffering from the cancer that had never quite left his body. I saw Hayes become crippled, both mentally and physically, from this evil disease. I saw some of the long-term side effects holding him back from progressing in life like his brother and sister. It felt as though we were delaying an ugly, inevitable moment. This weighed on my mind as we made our decision.

We were both on board to go through radiation treatments if it meant giving Hayes some sort of quality of life, free from a morphine state. We both wanted him to live as long as he could, regardless of the possible costs associated with it. We believe in miracles, so we weren't about to shut down any possible way to help our boy.

Hayes was starting to turn a corner. As the day passed, he became more alert and they began weaning him off the morphine.

We were so relieved to see some improvement. With Thanksgiving only a day away, the physicians were hopeful that that they'd be able to discharge Hayes in time for us to enjoy the holiday as a family. Not exactly how we envisioned it, but a chance to be at home together was extremely exciting.

21
THANKSGIVING

"They are letting us go home!" Savanna texted as I was at home with the kids on the evening of Thanksgiving. "I'm so excited." It's amazing how fast our emotions had changed in the past 24 hours. Getting Hayes home had become essential. We had received the most devastating news a parent could get, and we needed love and support from our family. It was fitting that it happened to be on Thanksgiving, quite possibly the last one as a family of eight.

The kids were thrilled to have all of us home. When Savanna walked in the door with Hayes, I observed him closely. He didn't look much healthier on the outside, so I was extremely anxious to see how he would do while home. For the first time since we had begun this fight, we felt intimidated by having him home. We were pretty experienced when it came to taking care of a sick child, but this felt much more serious. Morphine had been the only thing to tame his pain and we didn't have access to it at our home.

I was running on fumes, with only a few hours of sleep the entire week, but the kids needed a pick-me-up with all that had transpired. One of our annual traditions was to put up our Christmas tree on Thanksgiving night, and this year wasn't about to be an exception. So I pulled together any energy I had left and dragged the tree up from the basement. As I dragged the box that contained our twelve-foot tree (yeah, it's a bit excessive, but we love Christmas season at the Tate household), I could hear Hayes throwing up. His poor little body, withered from all the stress and abuse he had taken since coming home from Disneyland, was still in obvious pain. He barely had enough energy to hold his poor little head up, and his eyes were drooping from lack of sleep. It was apparent he needed some rest, so while Savanna started digging through the storage boxes for decorations, I got Hayes ready for bed and laid him down in his crib. In the crib beside him, Heath was already down for the night. Hayes immediately fell asleep.

Savanna and the kids were downstairs putting up the decorations. Savanna was doing her best to create some Christmas magic, as we had done every year since the kids were babies. She's always done an amazing job creating a fun house during the holidays. I waited a few minutes before leaving Heath and Hayes's room that night, because I admit that I had no desire to put up Christmas decorations—especially not the gigantic tree. With lack of sleep, I was due for some sort of Christmas meltdown. You know, the fit that every dad has during Christmas time? Feel free to visit our house in the coming years if you have never witnessed a true dad-holiday meltdown. I've been known to have a few, especially when it comes to faulty lights.

Beneath that, the real reason I hesitated to leave Hayes's room that night was because I felt that his body was breaking down. I felt as though I may never get another chance to put him in that crib again. I sunk onto the carpet in between their cribs and cried. I couldn't hold back. The tears were coming from a broken parent, who was witnessing his little boy suffer before his eyes. And that was just the beginning of the longest, most eventful night of our lives.

We did the best we could to create some Christmas magic that Thanksgiving night. By the end, even the kids were tired since their

Grandma had spoiled them by extending their usual bedtimes. We kissed them goodnight and went to bed. As Savanna and I walked by the baby boy's bedroom, we could hear Hayes moaning in pain. In between the moans, there was gagging. Savanna opened the door just enough for the light to shine on Hayes's face. I was right beside her as we walked to his crib. She reached down with both hands and picked him up to provide some motherly cuddles and comfort.

Hayes was covered in throw up. We were hesitant to turn on the light, to avoid waking Heath, but we needed to clean up his crib. I flipped the light switch and turned back to Savanna. Hayes was cuddled up in her arms, with his chest against hers, and he looked up at me, barely able to lift his head. I looked directly in those baby-blue eyes and did a double-take in disbelief. His right eye was completely off-center, deviating to his right side.

"What happened to his eye?" I asked in a panic, as if Savanna would have any idea what was going on.

"What do you mean?" she replied.

"It's totally unfocused. His right eye is lazy," I said as I pointed to his eye. Savanna looked and covered her mouth in horror.

Our beautiful baby, with eyes resembling an angel's, was now physically disabled from the evil cancer that was quickly consuming his body. This was extremely depressing. His eyes were his one way to communicate with us. Those eyes told stories. They were gorgeous, they had talked to me on the beach in California, they had thanked me. Those eyes spoke to me personally and they were now becoming destroyed. To say it was horrifying is an understatement.

With Hayes in her arms, Savanna began walking to the master bedroom. I followed closely behind, with Hayes looking at me over her shoulder with only his left eye. The other was completely off to the right. I tried to stay calm, but it was extremely difficult to look at him. Because I felt like I was letting him down. I couldn't remove this evil disease from his little body. I felt extreme guilt, as if I was responsible somehow, and I needed him to know that I would take it away if I could. But there was no way to relay the message to him.

Savanna laid him down on the bed while I reached for the iPad to play one of his favorite shows, hoping to distract him somehow. It had been a solution for us at the hospital, when he seemed uncomfortable and unable to relax. Even during Hayes's darkest days, with mouth sores coating his entire throat, he found some measure of joy and distraction in his shows. I propped the screen up on the pillow beside his head so that he could watch while laying down. When the music came on, he immediately became more alert as excitement filled his soul. His head rotated a little to get a better view. He then moved it several times, attempting to focus, but it wasn't the point of view impeding him. It was his right eye, suddenly serving no more purpose than if it were made of glass. I saw his confusion, not knowing what was going on or why he couldn't see the images on the screen. I could do nothing more than cry as I watched my little buddy laying there, unable to find relief from pain and discomfort.

He was still throwing up consistently, in thirty-minute increments. There was no use taking him back to his room, so we kept Hayes in our bed the entire night between me and Savanna. A towel acted as a landing zone for the vomit. I looked at Savanna periodically throughout the night and saw hope fading from her eyes. The possibility of gaining time with radiation therapy had brought some measure of it.

That night, nothing provided any relief to Hayes. It was unbearable to watch; it was the lowest point in my life. At one point, the bile he had been vomiting turned red. He was now throwing up blood. The stomach acid had even started to burn his little cheeks. There were moments when each gag of nausea made him scream out in pain. His eyes stared at Savanna and I each time he threw up, as if telling us that his time on earth was coming to an end.

All we could do that night was hold him and pray for some sort of relief. I prayed that entire night, both in my heart and out loud. I prayed for relief. I prayed for comfort. I asked God to send his angels down to help Hayes. I was finally relinquishing my desires, and giving in to God's. I prayed to understand his greater plan.

We both felt completely helpless, and we began to see that there was nothing more we could do for him. That night gave us perspective. Admittedly, it was a perspective that we didn't want or expect, but we saw firsthand just how aggressive this disease was. We were witnessing pain caused by the tumors throughout his spine and brainstem, and it allowed us to think as Hayes would. Hayes's body was failing him, his brain was being taken over. That night, I believe Hayes made a decision for the next step. And he let us know that he was done fighting.

After ten hours of complete suffering, we checked into the hospital for the last time. We walked through the ER doors for one purpose, and one purpose only—to provide comfort and relief from pain.

I had hit the anger stage in my emotional carousel. I wanted answers. With Hayes asleep in the hospital crib, I grabbed a dry-erase marker and wrote down the specific questions that I needed answers to.

Why is his eye now completely unfocused?

Will glasses fix this problem?

Why haven't we seen relief from nausea since the shunt surgery?

Is the shunt working properly?

Why is he in so much pain?

How are we going to manage his pain?

Is this a possible infection from the surgery?

I demanded these questions to be answered and expected to go through this list, one by one, until I felt comfortable with each topic. I wasn't going to protect anybody's feelings that day. I was so angry, I wasn't going down without a fight.

I sat on the windowsill in an impatient and extremely emotional state. The nurse would come in occasionally to check Hayes's vitals. We knew her from the previous six rounds of therapy. She had always been a good nurse for us. "Hey Sabrina?" I asked. "Could you page the oncology team for me?"

"Oh, they're outside," she said, surprised that they hadn't come in to talk to us. "Have they not come in yet?" she asked. "I figured they had already talked to you since they have been out there for the past thirty minutes," she said as she finished taking Hayes's temperature.

I immediately stood and walked over to the window to see what was going on. They were all huddled around the computer, staring attentively at the screen. I thought it was pretty odd. Savanna didn't seem too surprised or concerned by it. I paced around the room, and after a few more minutes, the team of physicians knocked lightly on the door before making their way inside. All three peered to their right to see the whiteboard full of the questions I had prepared for them.

"We see the questions that you wrote down," the oncologist said, pointing to the whiteboard. "I have every intention of going through those questions one by one, but I want to discuss the MRI that we have been studying. I've looked at the locations of the tumors in Hayes's brainstem," she said. "There is a tumor that is pressing up against the cranial nerve. This is the nerve that affects your eyes. The reason Hayes's eye is now off-center is because of that tumor. This is extremely telling of how aggressive the cancer is," she said, pausing before making one last point.

"Only a week ago, this tumor didn't seem to have much of an effect on him, but in only three days it has grown big enough to take control of his eye movement. Furthermore," she began in a quieter tone, "the tumor growth has continued towards the part of the brain that controls nausea. This is the cause for his pain and discomfort."

"So how do we relieve him from the nausea?" I asked.

She stood there with an expression that said it all. It was apparent that there would be no relief. "So we just keep him like this?" I asked, pointing toward Hayes. The question was more of an assumption than it was an actual question, but the oncologist felt she needed to say something in response.

"If he hasn't been able to feel relief when he's off the morphine, then our options are limited. The tumor is preventing his brain from performing the basic life skills."

"So if we choose radiation, how soon would you be able to see possible relief?" I asked.

"Well, assuming it works," her tone conveyed a lack of confidence, "it could take months before we see any relief."

"We just keep him like this? He just stays on morphine?" I said quickly, almost cutting her off before she finished her last sentence.

All she did to answer was nod her head. She was implying there was no possible way his body could get through radiation. I knew it as well, but I was making sure that I had all the information.

"We need some time to digest this information," I said, and they headed out the door.

As they closed it, I pointed toward Hayes and said to Savanna, "What the hell kind of life is that?"

It was a rhetorical question, obviously. Hayes was being kept in a vegetative state, asleep on morphine all day. *Is this what Hayes would want?* I asked myself. We were now prisoners of the hospital, depending on them to keep our son comfortable. The morphine was the only relief we could offer. There were moments when he would wake up and be alert, but those moments became less and less frequent as the day passed into late evening.

I felt like I needed to talk to the older kids about the news we had just received. The kids had spent the day at my brother's house, and I asked him to bring them to the hospital. I met them at the entrance and brought them up back to the fourth floor. The whole time, I was thinking and praying about the right words to say. I searched for analogies, metaphors, and various examples that I could possibly use to explain the real possibility that their brother may die.

It wasn't right that I had to have this discussion with my kids, but it needed to be done. I wanted to make sure they knew everything, because I feared future resentment if I was not open and honest about their little brother. When we entered the hospital room, they were excited to see Hayes. They then sat down on the floor and I pulled up a short stool to make sure my eyes were aligned with theirs. All three were quiet, sitting cross-legged on the cold, hard hospital floor. They were extremely attentive, all six eyes staring up at me.

I made one final attempt to find the right words in my head. I thought about the things that I liked hearing from others when they were providing support. *What gave me comfort?* I asked myself, and immediately realized that a simple message would be more impactful than any complex words of wisdom. The words "It's going to be okay" passed through my head, and I knew that was it. I needed to let my kids know that everything was going to be okay.

I began talking to them about the entire journey we had been through. I talked about all the incredible memories we had made this past year with Hayes. I talked about the dark moments during Hayes's tumor removal and chemotherapy. I reminded them of the hope and light that we found during those dark moments. "This whole year has been full of highs and lows. We have fought so hard to keep Hayes healthy. Right now, Hayes's cancer is extremely aggressive. It has taken over some important parts of his brain, and the doctors aren't sure if there is anything that can help him at this point," I explained.

"I know we have all feared a possible life without Hayes. I'm scared to think about life without Hayes, and I know you are scared to think about life without him too. It doesn't feel right to even think about. But I also want you to know that he will always be a part of our family, even if it's not here physically," I said. Like other Christians, we believe that we will see our loved ones again after we pass on from our time on earth. We believe in immortality, or life after death. I reminded the kids of this belief before explaining a real possibility: Hayes may return to Heaven in the near future. I then said:

"It will be okay."

Even though I wasn't sure how or why it would be okay, I felt like they needed to hear that, in that moment. I continued, "It's going to be okay to cry. It's going to be okay to smile and laugh. That's what Hayes has shown us. He taught us that it's okay to be happy and to smile, even during life's darkest moments. It's also okay to be sad and mad. It's okay to cry and yell. It's okay to do all of that. But please know that it's going to be okay," I said, looking at all three of them in the eyes. "We will get through this together, and we will learn to be okay together.

"There is nothing that will get in the way of our family, and Hayes will always be a part of this family." I got off the stool to sit between them and hugged each one of them. All three were in tears. Savanna continued to talk to them about Hayes's impact on each of them and his impact on the world. She painted an incredible picture of the things Hayes had taught each of us as he expressed the need to be Hayestough. She made a promise to the kids that we were always going to be there for each one of them. We were going to make sure they were okay.

We talked for almost two hours that night. Then I walked the kids down to the lobby, as Savanna and I were both spending the night with Hayes. We talked a lot that night, going in and out of sleep, but there was one candid conversation about what was in our future and Hayes's future. We had never talked like this before. Death had never been an option, as bringing it up was like some sort of jinx, like it was giving up or losing hope. So we completely avoided it. But that night, we talked about our possible future without our little boy. We both expressed our fears of life without him. We even talked about the extremely intimate details of the dying process. I couldn't believe we were actually talking about my son's funeral and possible burial site. We didn't hold back and, although the discussion was extremely painful, it needed to be addressed. We needed to arrive at an acceptance that our future together may be one that didn't physically involve our youngest triplet.

We held each other, crying, as we tossed and turned in the hospital bed. We sat and prayed together. We prayed for comfort for Hayes. We asked Him to remove the pain, but more specifically we said, "If this be thy will, please take Hayes without pain." That night, we both felt Hayes was extremely close to Heaven. There was a spiritual presence in the room all night, and one specific thing happened that we will never forget. One that gave me extreme peace and comfort as a dad.

Hayes was still throwing up and screaming in discomfort. The nurses were in and out of the room throughout the night, and Savanna and I made our way to and from his crib each time the pain became so intense that he awoke from morphine-aided sleep. At one point, we thought we were going to lose him.

I walked over to Hayes's crib just after he had received a dose of morphine. He was calm and alert. His eyes were open and staring toward me as I huddled over the railing. I could sense he was still in some pain, and my mind flooded with all the previous days and nights when I had cuddled him in his crib. My eyes teared up, and I spoke to Hayes: "Hayes," I said, with my eyes fixated on his, "I am sorry Hayes. I am so, so sorry." I moved my left hand over his forehead and rubbed his head back and forth, feeling his thick hair. His eyes were looking up at me, and he opened his mouth. With perfect annunciation and clarity, he said:

"It's okay."

I immediately looked at Savanna to confirm what just happened. Her eyes were wide and her jaw open in complete astonishment. Hayes had only ever been able to say a couple of words. He knew how to say "dog," which made us realize the impact our family pet had on Hayes, and occasionally he would say "dad." So there was no explanation for this. We had just witnessed a miracle.

It was exactly what I needed to hear from Hayes. Guilt had weighed on me the entire year because I was simply unable to make things better. I wanted nothing more in the world than to have him healthy, so my helplessness caused a profound heaviness. I had needed him to know that I would've done anything to take the pain away, if I only could. I needed him to know that I was sorry.

His simple response, "It's okay," was all I needed to hear. It will forever be carved in my brain.

We both stood in amazement and hunched over to hug him and kiss him on the forehead. It was amazingly refreshing to see him awake after being asleep for almost the entire day. As Savanna and

I leaned over him, with our eyes filled with tears and noses runny, we both told him, "We love you."

He looked back up at us and said, "I love you." Once again, those three words were uttered without hesitation and perfect enunciation.

We immediately looked at each other with gigantic smiles. Our tears rolled off our cheeks as we hugged each other. It was an incredibly happy moment. It's amazing to feel so much happiness in a moment of complete despair, but hearing Hayes's words was hearing a miracle. It was a tender mercy from Heaven. Another direct answer to our prayers.

It was such a gift to us since we would not be able to hear Hayes say those words for the remainder of our lives. Every parent deserves to hear their children express love and appreciation. Hayes had done just that. We never expected Hayes to speak to us, and I believe God knew we needed to hear him speak those words. Hayes knew that we needed to hear those words. That simple three-word phrase filled our hearts that night and helped comfort us when we needed it most. It didn't change our sadness or sorrow, but it provided a much-needed boost, an unexpected charge to our souls. The holes in our hearts were briefly filled.

There is no explanation for his words, but if one person could perform an inexplicable miracle, it was our little angel, Hayes. This was one of many miraculous things he had done in his brief life.

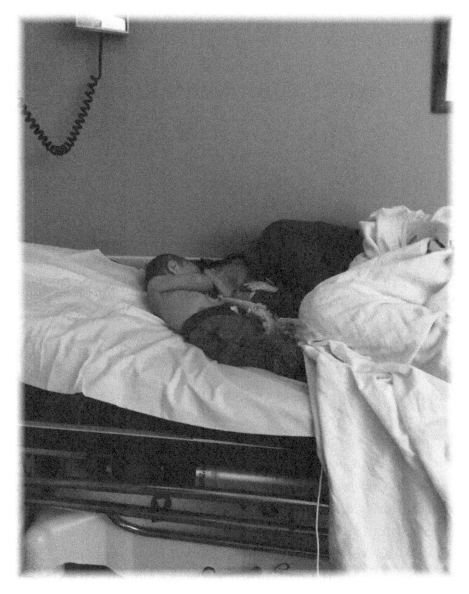

Hayes laying with Savanna during his final stay in the hospital.

22
WE'RE TAKING HIM HOME

The things we witnessed that night at the hospital were miracles. Through much of Hayes's treatments, Savanna and I had almost lost our ability to pray. We had both grown up in families that attended church regularly and had backgrounds in our religious beliefs. We were both active in our faith, but what does that mean, exactly?

I feel it's extremely easy to be faithful in your beliefs when things are going well. We had both been extremely blessed in our lives and there had never been an event that tested our faith. Hayes's diagnosis tested our faith and eventually our willingness to pray. We prayed often at the beginning, but there came a point when we felt many of our prayers were going unanswered. We prayed before the MRIs early on, and they never seemed to turn out as we had hoped or prayed for. We prayed each time Hayes was entering a crucial point in his treatments, hoping for relief from side effects. And we were so often disappointed that our faith was tested.

It weighed on the both of us. We became bitter with God for allowing this type of thing to happen to our little boy. But, can you blame us? If you find yourself judging us or blaming us for feeling bitterness or anger toward God, then you probably haven't been in our shoes. This bitterness was new in our lives and it certainly wasn't present all the time, but there were periods when we lost our faith in prayer. Our faith had been tested and perhaps we were faltering more than we imagined.

I had made a promise to myself and to God not to ask *Why?* because I knew there could never be a plausible explanation. There was no use asking God why this was happening in our lives, but I specifically did ask him to get us through it. There's really no way to quantify His assistance, especially the week we faced the ultimate nightmare: our son dying. My interpretation of "getting us through it" was giving Hayes a healthy life. It wasn't supposed to happen like this, and extreme anger filled me the entire week we spent watching helplessly while our little boy suffered. It filled me up until Hayes spoke to us. As we stood there in amazement, I could feel the bitterness leave my heart.

Suddenly, my bitterness was replaced with an extremely odd, but undeniable, sense of gratitude. *Why am I feeling gratitude? At a time like this?* I couldn't believe I was actually feeling some optimism in the darkest moment of my life. I was gaining the eternal perspective that I had lacked the entire year. And maybe it was precisely because I had been so preoccupied with being angry and bitter that I failed to understand the greater plan. A plan that consisted of seeing Hayes again after he dies. That dark November night, my faith was restored. There was no denying our conversation with Hayes, and it was—without a doubt—a modern-day miracle.

I sat down moments later and began to reflect on his entire life with us. I thought back to the original ultrasound when we couldn't hear his heartbeat. He wasn't supposed to have survived that week. In fact, the physician had informed us that it was perhaps better if he didn't, based on the risk increase to Savanna's health and that of the other babies. But Hayes beat the odds and fought to be a part of our family.

What would life have been like if we hadn't had a chance to meet Hayes? I wondered. *What if that black and white shadow that appeared on the ultrasound that day, whose heart wasn't yet beating, never joined our family?* Suddenly that thought became unbearable. I began thinking of the amazing lessons that Hayes had taught me in twenty months. I looked at his life, the example he gave us, and all the lives he had touched in his brief time on earth.

Earlier that day, I had posted an update on Hayes's condition on Instagram. The support and love that we had received this entire year from social media was beyond our imagination. Yes, we had felt compelled to share his journey with the world, but our definition of the world consisted of friends, family, and a few acquaintances. Okay, it may have consisted of some University of Utah fans and triplet enthusiasts—which, by the way, attracts a wide and strange audience. Initially, we weren't expecting much of a following, nor did we care about that at all. Our intention was to use social media as a simple way of relaying updates on Hayes. Sure, we had visions of becoming advocates of childhood cancer to raise awareness, but that was more of a dream than an expectation.

Hayes had a way of moving people, simply through his eyes and smile. People would see the images we posted and suddenly feel connected to him. It made for connections that multiplied with each and every post that we shared. The world was now following our story and loving our special little boy. Between all our accounts, the followers were reaching 80,000 people from hundreds of countries. At one point, Savanna and I began marking each country on a map hanging in our dining room.

These people followed our journey because of Hayes. They loved our little boy. They felt drawn to him, to his persona. I told you he had an angel's eyes, right? People from all demographics and backgrounds were now a part of Hayes's Army. His fight against cancer resonated with young and old alike. Religion and beliefs played no part in the reasons for following Hayes; they were part of his army because of the person he was. They were touched by a little boy fighting a grown-up disease with a smile on his face, laughing while he enjoyed life.

On November 26, I felt inspired to ask Hayes's followers to share the ways in which Hayes has impacted them. This was something that I needed to hear, directly, as I processed the likelihood of him passing away. The responses brought me to tears, in gratitude and pride. Here are a few of the thousands of responses that I received.

"I recently found out I am pregnant and my husband does not want this baby. I have filed for divorce and decided I would love nothing more but to name him or her after Hayes."

"I'm twenty-four, I have no religion, and I live all the way in Australia. I just wanted to tell you that your story has greatly impacted my life. Never before have I prayed, but each night before I go to sleep I pray that Hayes will have no more pain, I pray for your family."

"Hayes has taught me to be happy. Actual happiness. Happy with the ups and downs of life—no matter what, just keep fighting through."

"I have followed your journey since Hayes was diagnosed and I was three months pregnant. I battle serious mental illness and contemplated not keeping the baby. But Hayes changed that. He gave me hope during those dark days. I now have a beautiful three-month-old daughter."

"I'm a young, stay-at-home mom with two boys. My husband works long hours and while I'm so thankful that I'm able to stay home with my children, I find myself getting easily frustrated and overwhelmed. In those times, I think of Hayes and am reminded how precious their little lives are. He has made me a better mother to my own children. They will grow up remembering a fun, loving mother because of Hayes."

"Your son and all of the other children who have faced cancer helped me decide what career I want. I want to be a pediatric oncologist to help save children like yours. I have also learnt to cherish every moment I have in my life and make them worthwhile. Praying for your family."

"I stumbled upon your Instagram by fate. My heart physically aches, and I have found myself with tears in my eyes thinking "Why him?" He has taught me so many lessons, with the biggest being that I consider every single moment with my little babies a gift. No phones. No distractions. It's all about being present in the moment with them, and all family and friends."

"He is showing us that there is still so much love and compassion in world. He is giving me hope. So many people love him and your family. I felt as if he was one of my own. Feel proud, he is an angel, a warrior. He showed the grace of God in this world."

"Hayes has taught me to be a better dad. To cherish every moment with my kids and to take a deep breath instead of getting angry. Savanna and you have also taught me a lot about faith. To trust in our Heavenly Father and to seek His comfort. May God bless you two, Hayes, and your entire family. You are an example to all and I hope you can feel our love."

"Lil Hayes's journey has taught me to cherish every moment in life. I too am battling cancer and felt helpless many times—until I read Hayes's story. He has brought a lot of strength into my life."

"I am a fifteen-year-old Spanish girl and this child has taught me to value my family, to value every moment that I am with them. Hayes is strong and I sincerely write this with tears in my eyes... Give him a kiss on my part, I will be praying for him and his family. Kisses from Spain."

"I think Hayes has taught me to fall in love just through a picture, his cute face can just brighten my day and seeing him so sick makes me sad. He's one powerful, special baby to touch so many people's lives and hearts. Love from Scotland."

"We found out that we are expecting identical twin boys. We have been trying to find the perfect names for our boys, but it's been hard. We had decided that we wanted both of their names to start with the letter H. We both agreed on Hunter and we were still trying to come up with the second name when I came across an incredibly touching story about Hayes. I've been captivated by his strength and fight to live! He is a tough little guy who continues to fight and be so brave. I knew as soon as I read your story that Hayes was our second name. It had to be!"

These are only a few of the stories people wrote to us. How incredible is that? Hayes literally saved lives in his brief, impactful life. He was a miracle witnessed by hundreds of thousands of people on social media. My baby boy was not just special to me, he was special to the rest of the world.

His mission had become more apparent to me that night. *Hayes is a legend!* I thought to myself as I sat in the hospital bed. At one point Savanna, still with tears in her eyes, was huddling over his crib watching him rest, and I got up and walked over to her. As I walked towards her I said, "How lucky am I?" I felt extremely lucky to be Hayes's dad. The bitterness had ceased and the gratitude flooded my every thought as I reflected on his life and the impact he had on so many people.

Hayes continued to fight through the night and into the next morning. During that moment just after we told him we loved him, when we felt he wasn't going to make it, when we worried we might need to say our goodbyes that night, there was something extremely inhumane about being contained in a hospital room. If indeed Hayes was losing this battle, that room was too depressing and impersonal to say goodbye in. We were interrupted constantly by people checking his vitals. I don't think we necessarily accepted the fact that he was dying, but we were not naive enough to ignore the signs that there wasn't much time left in his brief life. And I'll be damned if that was how he would leave this world. Hayes had spent way too much time locked in that hospital room, and I didn't want his life to end in it. We made the decision to take him home that morning.

I wasn't really sure what the protocol was for taking him home from the hospital, but what the hell did I care? We were making a decision that was best for Hayes and our family. I knew the kids missed us and they missed Hayes. I also thought about their needs when we made this decision to bring him home. They were entitled to say their goodbyes and to cuddle him in the privacy of their own home. Bo had called me on the phone in tears to say, "Dad, I miss you guys." I knew they missed us, and we missed them. I was extremely proud of our kids for the way they fought alongside Hayes the entire year. They never complained, even though they had every right to complain about the situation.

We called the oncology team that morning and asked to be released from the hospital. It was an extremely difficult decision, even though we knew it was the right thing to do. The word "hospice" triggered all kinds of emotions, and just saying it made me cringe. I could tell the doctors had been trained extremely well to not try and persuade people one way or another on this decision. I understood why, but I also felt like I needed some sort of direction. I needed confirmation that we were making the right decision, and so I prayed to God for some sort of answer.

Then there was a knock at the door from a physician we didn't recognize. He looked in the window and asked, "Can I come in?" He was wearing a badge that we couldn't quite read until he was in the room. He was an oncologist who happened to be on call that weekend, but he had never met us, nor Hayes, since we began treatments. That was odd, given the fact that we were regulars on the floor.

"I heard you were thinking about taking Hayes home," he said. He talked about the fight that we had all just endured during six rounds of therapy. Then his eyes swelled with tears as he said, "I have never been in your shoes as a parent. But I felt a need to come talk to you today, as both a dad and as a physician, in hopes of giving you some relief in your decision to take Hayes home." He talked about how the fight against cancer is often referred to as a "battle," and what's lost in a battle is any peace and comfort. "Your fight isn't being relinquished or given up," he said. "You are now fighting for peace and comfort. Which, to me, is much more noble and courageous as a parent." He continued with one last thought: "It's not the easiest decision as a parent, but it's the right one for Hayes."

I have never been more appreciative of honesty than in that moment. He spoke directly to my soul. I cried the entire time he was talking, feeling its impact deeply. I wanted to stand up and hug him, but I refrained myself. I did, however, thank him from the bottom of my empty heart. Although our interaction with this physician was brief, I have no doubt that he was put in our path. It wasn't by some random chance that he happened to be assigned to us that day. He was there to give us direction and confirmation on one of the most important decisions of our lives. He was an answer to our prayers.

I stood up, hugged him, and wiped the tears from my cheek. Now Savanna and I both knew that we were making the right choice. We were taking our little boy home on hospice. I hate the word "hospice," so I'll say that again. We were taking our little boy home to live in peace and comfort with our family for the remainder of his life. That sounds way better.

Hayes was in pretty bad shape. His poor body was severely beaten up from a week of nonstop vomiting. He was now completely reliant on morphine to relieve pressure from the fluid that built up in his head. Due to the severity of the tumors in his brainstem, the fluid was too much for the shunt to be able to work as it should. The tumors were preventing drainage in his brain, so the only way he could find any relief was to throw up. The pain was unbearable for even Hayes, the toughest of kids. The short, fifteen-minute drive home took hours of preparation to make sure a last dose of morphine was given to him just as we walked out the door.

With discharge papers in hand, we made our final exit out the hospital doors. We had said our goodbyes to so many incredible people, including the nurses who had spent long hours playing with Hayes in the middle of the night. He completely charmed them, as Hayes was a little bit of a flirt. And he had become a celebrity, not just in the cancer unit, but throughout the entire hospital. So many people had gotten to know our little boy and cared for him with incredible compassion and love. Nurses and doctors made their way toward us for one final goodbye.

Hayes was in Savanna's arms wearing a beanie that a volunteer had knitted for him. It was a green beanie, perfect for Hayes, and strands of hair peeked through the side of it. We were really proud of his hair. It served as a trophy, won after fighting through intense chemotherapy. Hayes was also proud of his hair. There were times when he would let his little hands wander up onto the top of his head to move his hair back and forth with curiosity. I could tell that he loved the way it felt.

He was alert as we made a final walk down through the main hospital entrance. His cheeks were red, as he was still recovering from acidic burns from all the vomiting. His body was frail, hardly able to support itself as he sat his bum on Savanna's arm, his chest against hers in classic toddler form. Walking out those doors was the first of many "last times" for Hayes.

As we loaded him in our suburban for the last time, and strapped him into his car seat for one last time, we both cried out loud. It took us a while to leave the parking lot. We began talking about an unbearable thought: moving forward in life without our boy. It was really hitting me hard. I peeked back to see him hunched over in his little car seat. We talked about the upcoming Christmas season without him, and the trip that we had planned for late January to Hawaii.

"We can't go without him," I said to Savanna as my voice got higher. "It just doesn't feel right." Savanna was silent, unable to speak through the flood of emotions. Then a song came on the radio: "I Will Follow You" by Toulouse.

I will follow you

Follow you wherever you may go
There isn't an ocean too deep
A mountain so high it can keep
Keep me away
Away from my love

I love you
I love you
I love you

Where you go, I follow
I follow
I follow

You'll always be my true love
My true love
My true love
Forever

I will follow you

Every since you touched my hand, I knew
Near you, I always must be
Nothing can keep you from me
You are my destiny

I love you
I love you
I love you

I love you
I love you
I love you

Where you go, I follow
I follow
I follow

You'll always be my true love
My true love
My true love
Forever

I will follow you

Follow you wherever you may go
There isn't an ocean too deep
A mountain so high it can keep
Keep me away
Away from my love

While the song played, everything came to a sudden stop: our emotions, fears, and regrets. Afterward, we looked at each other as we thought the same thing. Hayes was telling us that he was going to be with us, not only during the holidays and our upcoming trip to Hawaii, but for the rest of our lives. That song came on to let us know that Hayes will follow us wherever we go.

The drive home was memorable. We pulled onto our street to see green ribbons wrapped around the fenceposts and utility poles. There were signs that read "Hayestough" on the neighbors' lawns. They came out to the street to wave as we made our way up the circle toward our house. There, we were greeted by both of our families standing on the front porch. Savanna held Hayes in her arms as we walked through a tunnel-like entrance, filled with embraces from each of them. They had been with us throughout this fight, and here they stood again.

23

WE LOVE YOU HAYES

$\mathcal{H}$ayes was home! This is where he was intended to be. It felt so good to have him there, surrounded by the people he loved and those who loved him. No longer confined in that hospital, where he had spent 140 days in less than a year.

I never imagined bringing Hayes home for his last days, but there was a peace in our home that evening that brought so much comfort to our family. We spent much of the evening with family and close friends as some of them said their goodbyes. Hayes was awake and so sweet, with his eyes half open as he was passed from person to person in our living room. Each one of them spent some time hugging and kissing our little boy. There were so many caring exchanges that took place, and every one was filled with love. There was one moment when it became extremely silent, and it was obvious the people in the room felt extreme concern for me, Savanna, and the kids. I felt a need to talk to them, to let them know some of the inspiring things that had occurred in the past few days.

"I wanted to share with you some the things that I have been feeling these past couple of days," I said to them, as twenty pairs of tear-filled eyes stared back at me. "There have been so many emotions this past week. We have been angry, sad, depressed, confused, and bitter," I said, taking a long breath before continuing. "I have also felt incredible pride and gratitude for being the dad of one of the most amazing boys in the world." I paused to wipe my eyes. "It's easy to have a heart filled with anger and bitterness, but I've asked myself what Hayes would want. I've thought a lot about what he has taught me in his twenty months on earth. He's taught all of us to smile in times of despair. He never let those moments define him. He smiled and laughed and enjoyed every moment, despite facing life's most difficult circumstances. Hayes taught me to embrace challenges. He taught me it's okay to smile. It's okay to be happy when perhaps there appears no reason to be happy."

The tears stopped for a moment as I offered my final thought: "Hayes has taught me that it'll be okay. We will be okay, because that's what he has taught us and that's what he would want."

At the same time, I wasn't naïve. I knew the next few days were going to be extremely difficult. But I felt the need to be strong, like Hayes, for my family so that we could all enjoy however much time we had left with him. I didn't want anyone to feel depressed. After all, that's why we left the hospital to be at home.

In the final days, we spent each and every minute with Hayes by our side. His crib had been set up next to our bed, but it was more of a decoration since he was either in our bed or in our arms the entire time. The kids got to spend incredibly valuable time with their little brother. They would stay up late with us, talking about the amazing things that he had taught us in his short life. We talked about the how different life would've been without him or the other babies.

At one point, Bo said, "Our family wasn't as close before the triplets came. I didn't feel as close to you then as I have since they were born." That was a special thing for me to hear, considering my old fears that the older kids might resent the babies. I had worried that they might feel as if they had taken a back seat, or that perhaps we had forgotten about them.

What Bo said was true. Hayes brought our family closer together. He taught us how to love each other, not in ways that center on superficial things, rather he taught us a love that is built on service. He taught us each how to be compassionate and caring. We learned to be a family built on selflessness. We had become a cohesive team built around one cause: helping Hayes. Now, I had been a part of some incredibly successful football teams. I was a part of the 2004 Fiesta Bowl team that became the first "mid major" to reach a BCS bowl game. They nicknamed us the "BCS Busters" because of the mountain we climbed to reach an unthinkable, undefeated season. During that season, Coach Urban Meyer spent many hours talking about the sum of the parts rather than the individuals themselves. We referred to our team as a family and we shared a family-like bond. We learned to be selfless players that year, as we focused solely on winning. I believe that was the main reason for our success that season. And it laid the foundation for the University of Utah to become part of the Pac-12 with the success that followed.

So I knew, as I sat there with my six kids, just how incredibly blessed I was. I was a part of something special. Although we were going through the most difficult time in our lives, my family had grown inseparable. This is why I knew we were going to be okay. I also knew Hayes was going to direct us in the future. He had already performed miracles during his time here on earth, and I had no doubt that he would continue to watch over us in Heaven.

Each night, as we sat with Hayes, the kids grew emotional at the thought of moving forward without him. I felt as though every night I had to give them a pep talk about the condition of their little brother. It was hard for them to grasp why he wouldn't be able to just wake up and be the Hayes they grown accustomed to seeing. I had to remind them of the status of his tumors and the aggressiveness of his cancer. It seemed like I was giving the same talk every night, but no matter how many times I gave that same speech, it never got easier. Tears would fill my eyes. My dad duties had never been more important than these days with my kids. They asked difficult questions, some of which I didn't know the answer to, but I did my best to keep it simple and remind them of my love for them. I kept reassuring them that our family was going to be okay, as Hayes would soon be our guardian angel.

Everyone seemed extremely heavy with emotions, so one night I asked each of the kids to plan an activity that they wanted to do to celebrate Hayes. I wanted them to think of something he would enjoy doing, or find joy in, as he looked down on us from his soon-to-be home, Heaven. "I want you each to plan an activity that we can do as a family to honor Hayes," I said to them as they looked at me with grins on their faces. It was something they were really excited to do, so they wasted no time throwing ideas at me.

Wes holding Hayes as he comes home to spend the remaining days with his family.

Mia wanted to visit the lights at Temple Square in downtown Salt Lake City. Temple Square is a main tourist attraction here, where a Mormon Temple is located. It is also the place where Savanna and I were married. During the Christmas season, they decorate the garden and trees in beautiful Christmas lights and nativity scenes. People come from all over the United States to visit it and our family has gone every holiday season. In fact, the previous year it had been our last family outing before we found out that Hayes had cancer.

Bo wanted to have a party for Hayes. He wanted to celebrate Hayes by having family and friends come over, including Santa. He also wanted to light Chinese lanterns and release them into the air as a way of sending wishes to Hayes in Heaven. Every Christmas Eve, our family lights these lanterns to send Santa Clause our Christmas wishes. "This year we can send our wishes to Hayes," Bo said.

When I asked Wes what he wanted to do to celebrate Hayes, he said, "I want to write letters to Hayes."

All three of them had incredibly thoughtful ways of paying tribute to their little brother. It was a way for them to do something fun so they could smile while thinking of him. While we sat there, planning these activities, the kids took turns talking to their little brother. Hayes had been asleep for almost the entire day, but he started to move his head around a little bit. His eyes were still closed as he reached around for a pacifier that had fallen out of his mouth. The kids were really excited to see him awake.

"We love you Hayes!" they said in perfect unison.

"We love you Hazers!" "Hazers" was the kid's nickname for him.

They said it one more time: "Hazers, we love you!"

Hayes was still half-awake, moving his head back and forth, when suddenly he pulled his pacifier out of his mouth. With his eyes still closed, he said, "I love you."

Each one of our jaws dropped, and everyone's eyes were wide. We couldn't believe what he had just heard. Even Savanna and I, despite the fact that we had heard him speak a few days before. All three of the kids looked at each other in astonishment. They giggled with joy as one of them said in excitement, "Did you just hear that?"

It was one of the more precious moments that the kids experienced. For them to experience this, the same miracle as Savanna and I had witnessed in the hospital, was an answer to our prayers. It completely validated our decision to bring Hayes home to be with his family.

This week happened to be the same week that ESPN was promoting cancer research through the V Foundation, which was named after Jimmy Valvano—an extremely successful collegiate basketball coach who passed away from cancer in 1993. Every year, ESPN devotes the entire week to raising money by portraying six people currently battling cancer. Earlier in the summer, we had received a phone call from an ESPN representative informing us of their desire to showcase Hayes as one of the cancer fighters. They had come across our Instagram accounts and felt a connection with Hayes. They wanted to feature him as a portrayal of childhood cancer.

I was extremely honored to have Hayes represent the children currently fighting cancer. I watched Jimmy Valvano's now-legendary speech live, when I was nine years old. So having my son featured on ESPN for such an incredible cause made me proud. Never had I imagined that my family would become part of that world, as the victim and the voice. It was surreal.

While I watched pictures and videos of my strong little boy on ESPN, I posted on Twitter: "That's my son! Twenty months of age, yet Hayes has made an impact on this world that most people don't do in a lifetime. How lucky am I?" Hayes was part of the greater cause to perhaps one day find a cure for this evil disease. I felt so much pride and joy as a dad that night. My son was a legend, and despite the heartache that I was feeling given the circumstances, I couldn't have felt more lucky to call him my son.

Seeing Hayes on ESPN also helped me realize how incredible his mission in life had been. It was one of the things that I talked about with the kids during those last nights with Hayes. "There will be a time in your lives when you realize just how amazing your little brother was. Right now, you might be a little too young to understand the impact he has had on people's lives, but someday people will refer to you as 'Hayes's brother' or 'Hayes's sister.'"

I felt the need to tell them that because I had already been introduced to people as "Hayes's dad." I was no longer the Steve Tate who played football at the University of Utah. I wasn't even the guy who had triplets. I was now Steve Tate, the guy who had Hayes as a son.

The legend of Hayes was felt all that week, as love and support poured in from across the world. We received hundreds of cards and packages from people who only knew us through social media. We received a package from the United Emirates that contained toys, T-shirts, and stuffed animals. It was labeled "To Master Hayes," and it cost $200 just to ship. Packages came from Norway, France, and India. We weren't standing alone in this fight, and the gifts demonstrated just how incredible Hayes's impact was on this world. This helped offset much of the pain that we had to endure that week.

On December 3, our pain hit an all-time high when we were told that Hayes probably wouldn't survive the remainder of the day. When the nurse came by to check on Hayes, he noticed that his breath was slowing and his heartrate was increasing. "All signs are pointing to this afternoon or evening," he said to us with a soft tone. It was extremely hard to hear. We had been living an emotional rollercoaster the entire week, which included moments of denial in which we thought that he was going to somehow beat it and miraculously sit up to play.

Our extended family spent the entire day with the babies and cleaning around the house. Savanna and I didn't leave Hayes's side that day, not even for food. We wanted to be there for every minute of his life. We didn't want to stop caring for our little boy or fighting next to him. We wanted his body to feel clean and fresh, so we gave him a bath. We washed his little hands and feet, and shampooed his blonde hair one last time.

It was getting late, approaching 10 p.m., and the nurse called to check in with us. When he anticipated only a few hours left, he showed how little he knew our Hayes. Such a fighter wasn't going to leave his family without defying some sort of odds. The babies and Wes were asleep in their rooms. Bo and Mia were with Savanna and I, in our bedroom, taking turns holding Hayes and soaking in every remaining minute with him. From the foot of the bed, I observed the unique presence in the room. It was profoundly peaceful, much more so than any other night that week. There was a tremendous warmth pervading the silence. The kids had given Hayes their nightly kisses, and handed him back to Savanna. I was about to say something to Bo and Mia, when suddenly Savanna said:

"Steve…he's going on." She was looking down at the fading pulse in Hayes's neck. I moved toward the two of them. Hayes gave two final, deep breaths, and passed away peacefully in Savanna's arms. He was gone.

Everything was quiet and calm. The comforting warmth surrounded us, as we sat there with Hayes's body. Tears flowed from each pair of eyes, but we felt extremely peaceful. The only experience I can compare it to is the moment when a baby is born. A Heavenly presence surrounded us.

We spent the next hour with Hayes. We cried, and we smiled as we kissed him. We held his little hand and begged him to visit us. I asked him to watch over his brothers and sisters. I promised him that I would make him extremely proud by keeping his legacy alive. I told him I loved him, and gave him one last kiss.

Then they arrived to take Hayes away. When they rang the doorbell, I answered, and immediately asked them to allow me to take him to the car. I wanted to be the one to take him away that night. I walked slowly upstairs to get my baby boy from Savanna's arms. I held him close to my chest as Savanna passed him to me. His frail little body was motionless in my arms as I made my way down the hall, toward the stairs, and eventually out the front door. Savanna followed, and wrapped her arms around my shoulders as we put him in the black van and secured his little body. We hugged each other for a few seconds before making our way to the front porch. Then we watched them drive away.

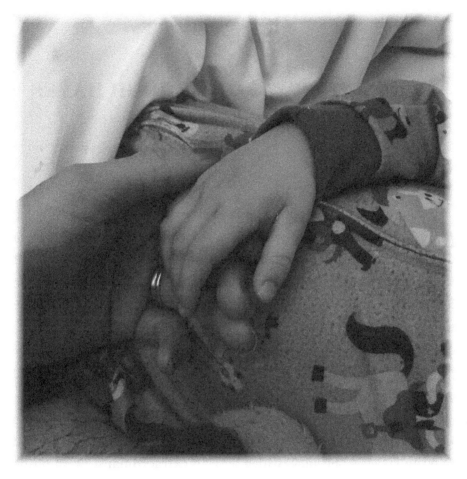

Hayes holds Savanna's hands just prior to passing away.

24
MOVING FORWARD THROUGH HAYES

*A*n excruciating amount of grief followed the next morning, and it came in waves throughout the week. There was a lot to get done, so we didn't have much time to sit and cry. We didn't want to let anything get in the way of preparing for a day of celebration for Hayes. I have always hated the sadness at funerals. I obviously understand why it's a sad event, but I always felt it should be an occasion to celebrate the life of a loved one. So that's what we planned to do for Hayes. We were determined to make it a special day, in which we celebrated and honored Hayes's amazing life.

I spent much of the next day sitting down with my kids to write their funeral talks, while Savanna planned the details. I also had to write Hayes's obituary, which was an extraordinary intimidating thing to do. There aren't any classes that teach you how to do this. And this was something that I wanted to be perfect. *How am I supposed to sum up his impactful life in just a few paragraphs?* I thought to myself as I sat at my desk. I turned on the computer and began writing. Words and thoughts flowed from my mind. It was almost effortless, I was so inspired to write about my angelic little boy.

We hadn't had much time to reflect back on the previous year, but Savanna and I knew there were two ways to behave as we moved forward and coped with this tragedy. We could become bitter, mad, and allow those emotions to control our actions for the remainder of our lives—which would teach our children to behave that way too.

Or, we could apply the amazing things that Hayes taught us, and use that as fuel to continue his legacy. We chose not to let tragedy define us. We were both determined to live our lives for Hayes.

"How would Hayes be living if he were still with us?" we asked ourselves. He certainly wouldn't be depressed or mad or bitter. Hayes taught us to shine in moments of darkness. He taught us to embrace the challenges with a smile. Hayes laughed at fear and pain. Never once did he allow those things to prevent him from enjoying his life here on earth, and I wasn't about to either.

As I wrote that obituary and my funeral talk, I kept thinking about the voice inside our heads that often tells us, "Life isn't fair, we don't deserve this." Whether or not that voice is something we are born with, it does become more persuasive as we get older, and we allow it to take over way too often. I thought about the fact that Hayes never allowed that voice to win. He never fell victim to it, so I was determined to do the same in my life moving forward.

I was inspired in a moment when perhaps I should have been sad. I immediately knew this was Hayes's doing. He was replacing depressing emotions with inspiration and motivation. I was already feeling his presence.

The business of the week made it fly by and the funeral day was quickly upon us. It was a cold Friday morning in December. Snow flurries were predicted for much of the day. The kids were dressed nice and warm, and all three were excited to talk about their little brother, sharing the thoughts they had written down. Savanna looked gorgeous as ever, with a quiet and calm presence. We all had some nerves that morning, but we also felt an excitement to honor our little fighter.

When we arrived at the church that morning, we found a congregation of more than 1,500 people. Our little family shared some of our memories of Hayes with this larger family, some that were extremely personal. There were tears shed, but there were also smiles and laughs. The musical numbers were extremely moving and caused me to cry as I rewound much of the past year through my mind. Savanna's concluding remarks set the tone:

I want to tell you, Hayes's story is still a miracle. He still gives me hope. Hayes is still smiling, and now he is cheering me on! I love him so much, but rather than feel angry, I honestly feel lucky. I don't know why I got so blessed. If there is any advice I can give you from this experience, it's to tell your story. Live your beautiful life and love your children. Thank you for letting me share the gift that Hayes was to the world. I feel incredibly humbled. Hayes's life and my life will always be connected. His life has no end. He is as real today as the day we found his perfect, teeny heartbeat in that ultrasound. Hayes is still life!

Prior to my talk, I played an audio clip of Hayes laughing over the sound system. I felt compelled to share it to remind people what Hayes was all about. He was about laughter and joy. He wouldn't have wanted us to cry, so I reminded the congregation of that just before I delivered my message to them. Here is part of it.

Hayes taught us to live each day as if it was a gift.
Hayes taught us to enjoy the small things in life.
Hayes taught us how to smile in life's scariest moments.

It's only fitting that we discuss the gift of a baby that would change the world during this Christmas season. A baby whose life impacted thousands. A baby who spoke not with his words, but with his divine spirit. His soul was old. He was wise. His baby blue eyes told a story. He was out of this world. He lived. He fought to live each day, and we fought with him.

As one person put it "Hayes was the best teacher I have ever had." He taught us how to overcome challenges. He taught us how to be Hayestough. What does it mean to be Hayestough? Hayestough is not a matter of being scared, but rather facing adversity head on despite being fearful. Hayestough is not about simply "enduring." It's about living in the moment and finding the joy in even the darkest situations. Hayestough isn't just about toughness, it's about love and purity. It's about smiles and giggles. Hayestough is about caring and nurturing. It's about selflessness and hope.

This was Hayes's mission on earth. A mission that was chosen prior to his coming. A mission to inspire others to live each day to the fullest, to inspire others and find courage in moments of despair. He was fulfilling his plan and telling his story. A story that needed to be told. His impact is felt and will continue to be felt as we carry on his legacy. A legacy that entails being tough in times of fear. One that entails overcoming life's biggest challenges. In some euphoric way, Hayes journey paved the way for me and our family to be able to endure this dreaded moment when he is no longer with us on earth, but rather in spirit. We are being Hayestough.

Hayes, I need to thank you for being the greatest gift I have ever received. Thank you for teaching us what true love feels like. A love that is based on service. Thank you for teaching me compassion. Thank you for allowing me to care for you, but more importantly... thank you for caring for me. You taught me how to be dad. You brought our family closer and you gave us a bond that will never be broken. A bond that will get us through the void that you left. We will be okay. Until we meet again, Hayes...

There was a feeling of hope and completion in the room. Our little boy's mission on earth was complete, and our new hope was focusing around the continuation of his legacy.

We concluded the gathering and made our way toward the parking lot so we could head to the burial ceremony. The funeral was in a large chapel with drapes covering each window for privacy, so we were unaware of the weather conditions. I assumed that we would find a parking lot full of snow. As we made our way outside, we walked into blue skies and sunshine, with a temperature in the mid-fifties. If you've ever been to Utah in December you'll understand that this is an incredible anomaly, only possible through the determination of our special little boy. Hayes had his way up in Heaven that day.

Sun shining on Hayes during a morning in December.

The sun continued to shine throughout the entire burial ceremony. I then handed out sixty green balloons to the people gathering around the casket, particularly the children. It was our salute to Hayes. I counted out loud to three, we said "Hayestough!" in unison, and then released all the green balloons to Heaven.

And the celebration continued. We held a "Hayes Happy Party" that night to fulfill Bo's wish to celebrate Hayes with a party that included both sets of family. We crammed forty people in the house to enjoy each other's company. We sat around eating pizza, sharing Hayes stories, and even had a visit from Santa Clause, which the kids loved. He even showed up wearing a "Hayestough" T-shirt under his red coat. That special night ended with a lantern ceremony. We lit Chinese lanterns and sent them into the air, sending our wishes to Hayes.

Santa pays a visit in his Hayestough T-shirt.

As family and friends were making their way out of the house that night, a friend of ours excitedly gasped while looking at her phone. She said, "I posted the video of the balloon ceremony on Facebook, and I've received several messages about an orb. Apparently there is a green orb toward the end of the video that follows the balloons into the air." She spoke a bit hesitantly, not knowing exactly what an orb was.

I had never heard of an orb either, so I searched on my phone for a definition or meaning. I came across an article that read, "Green orbs are sometimes thought to be an indication of the presence of a human spirit."

With my curiosity peaked, I pulled the video up on the television screen so everyone could see this supposed green orb. There it was! My eyes were wide open with my jaw dropped in amazement. I wasn't the only one with that reaction, as we all looked up and saw the same thing. We replayed the video at least ten times, each time following the circular green orb as it moved with the balloons in a seemingly excited state. There was a halo-like glow surrounding the green orb as it moved around the television screen. I had never seen anything like it before in my life. Of all the colors it could've been, it was green.

Two different cameras caught that same image during the balloon ceremony, ruling out any possible theory about a particular camera or lens. It was Hayes. He was sending us a sign to let us know he was okay.

We now refer to these moments as "Hayes Hints." They are the various signs that he gives us, letting us know he is always with us, staring down at us with his angelic baby blue eyes. He is a legend!

Families are forever.

ACKNOWLEDGMENTS

I have so many people to thank, who each contributed in some way through the course of this entire journey. I will start by thanking Hayes. Hayes, you taught me to love. You inspired me to write this book and opened doors to make this entire thing possible. I have no doubt that you have been with me through each step since I awoke in the middle of the night with the inspiration to write this story. You guided me each morning and evening as I sat with the other five kids, trying my best to make you proud.

I need to acknowledge my other kids: Bo, Mia, Wes, Heath, and Reese. My heart aches for the loss of your brother, which was a big factor in my decision to write this story. I want you to have a book full of the memories we shared together. I also want to inspire each of you to do hard things. You can accomplish anything you put your minds to. You have given me love, support, and the strength to continue each day. Without all of you, I am not sure I would be able to wake up each morning. You have given me life and purpose. I see Hayes in each one of you and it's evident that his legacy continues through you. I love you all so much.

To our neighbors who brought us meals each day to make sure that our kids were fed, I want to thank you from the bottom of my heart. I need to thank my family and Savanna's family for helping with the babies while I was at work and at the hospital. My mom came each morning at 7 a.m. to feed the babies while I got the kids ready for school. Those early mornings don't go unnoticed. Mom, I am blessed to have your love and support. The kids were so loved while they were hanging out with Grandma TT.

Thank you Krista Parry. You have been a Godsend in our lives. We are so grateful to have you as our friend.

Special thanks to Post Hill Press, Jennifer Holder, and the amazing people that made this book possible. They saw the potential for this unique story and gave me the opportunity to bring my story to the rest of the world. I was a complete rookie when it came to writing yet, with your help, I wrote a book that is now published!

I want to thank Dan Chipman for our friendship and his willingness to read over each chapter and offer his opinion. In addition, I need to thank Dan Marshall. You inspired me early on to write this book. And, despite the fact that you are a big-time author, you always offered assistance when needed and proofread the manuscript when it was finished.

Sincere gratitude goes out to the staff at Primary Children's Hospital. You cared for my son as if he was your own. We became family on the fourth floor, as you were so supportive and loving to us and Hayes. Thank you for loving our boy.

And to Hayes's Army from all over the world, who supported us through social media. We would read each comment and the love lifted us up during dark times. We continue to feel lifted up by each of you. You cared for a family and a little boy, despite not knowing him personally. You are "part of the good."

To my wife, Savanna. I am madly in love with you. I knew we had a special relationship since the day I met you at age eleven, but I can honestly say that my love for you only get stronger. You have always believed in me, despite my crazy ideas. You believe I can do anything and cheered me on while I wrote this book. You have always been my biggest fan and nobody believes in me more than you. I love you babe. Thank you for being mine.

ABOUT THE AUTHOR

Steve Tate grew up in Salt Lake City, Utah, where he attended the University of Utah and served as an All-Conference captain as a strong safety for the football team. He married his high school sweetheart, Savanna Thompson, at the young age of 21.

Steve and his wife found out they were expecting triplets to join their current family of three children: Bo, Mia, and Wes. Their children Reese, Heath, and Hayes were born in 2015. Hayes was diagnosed with a rare form of brain cancer in January 2016. After almost a year of battling through numerous rounds chemotherapy and a stem cell transplant, Hayes returned to his Heavenly Father on December 3, 2016.

After losing his son, Steve felt inspired and decided to honor him by writing a book. Steve and his wife continue to be huge childhood cancer advocates through the Hayestough foundation, where they focus on helping families battling cancer and raising funds for research. They actively work with members of Congress to raise awareness and funding for children with cancer. They remain engaged through their various social media platforms.